OPPOSING
VIEWPOINTS®
SERIES

Transportation

Other Books of Related Interest:

Opposing Viewpoints Series

Government Spending

Global Resources

Current Controversies Series

Pollution

The Middle East

At Issue Series

Foreign Oil Dependence

What Is the Impact of Automation?

"Congress shall make
no law . . . abridging
the freedom of speech,
or of the press."

First Amendment to the U.S. Constitution

The basic foundation of our democracy is the First Amendment guarantee of freedom of expression. The Opposing Viewpoints Series is dedicated to the concept of this basic freedom and the idea that it is more important to practice it than to enshrine it.

Transportation

Louise Gerdes, Book Editor

GREENHAVEN PRESS

A part of Gale, Cengage Learning

GALE
CENGAGE Learning™

Detroit • New York • San Francisco • New Haven, Conn • Waterville, Maine • London

Christine Nasso, *Publisher*
Elizabeth Des Chenes, *Managing Editor*

© 2008 Greenhaven Press, a part of Gale, Cengage Learning.

Gale and Greenhaven Press are registered trademarks used herein under license.

For more information, contact:
Greenhaven Press
27500 Drake Rd.
Farmington Hills, MI 48331-3535
Or you can visit our Internet site at gale.cengage.com

For product information and technology assistance, contact us at

Gale Customer Support, 1-800-877-4253
For permission to use material from this text or product, submit all requests online at www.cengage.com/permissions

Further permissions questions can be emailed to permissionrequest@cengage.com

Articles in Greenhaven Press anthologies are often edited for length to meet page require-ments. In addition, original titles of these works are changed to clearly present the main thesis and to explicitly indicate the author's opinion. Every effort is made to ensure that Greenhaven Press accurately reflects the original intent of the authors. Every effort has been made to trace the owners of copyrighted material.

Cover photograph reproduced by permission of Rokusek Design, Inc.

LIBRARY OF CONGRESS CATALOGING-IN-PUBLICATION DATA

Transportation / Louise Gerdes, book editor.
 p. cm. -- (Opposing viewpoints)
 Includes bibliographical references and index.
 ISBN-13: 978-0-7377-3830-8 (hardcover)
 ISBN-13: 978-0-7377-3831-5 (pbk.)
 1. Transportation--United States--Juvenile literature. 2. Transportation and state--United States--Juvenile literature. I. Gerdes, Louise I., 1953-
 HE152.T68 2008
 388.0973--dc22
                                                        2008006565

Printed in the United States of America
1 2 3 4 5 6 7 12 11 10 09 08

Contents

Chapter 3: What Laws Best Protect Driver Safety?

Why Consider Opposing Viewpoints?

> *"The only way in which a human being can make some approach to knowing the whole of a subject is by hearing what can be said about it by persons of every variety of opinion and studying all modes in which it can be looked at by every character of mind. No wise man ever acquired his wisdom in any mode but this."*
>
> John Stuart Mill

In our media-intensive culture it is not difficult to find differing opinions. Thousands of newspapers and magazines and dozens of radio and television talk shows resound with differing points of view. The difficulty lies in deciding which opinion to agree with and which "experts" seem the most credible. The more inundated we become with differing opinions and claims, the more essential it is to hone critical reading and thinking skills to evaluate these ideas. Opposing Viewpoints books address this problem directly by presenting stimulating debates that can be used to enhance and teach these skills. The varied opinions contained in each book examine many different aspects of a single issue. While examining these conveniently edited opposing views, readers can develop critical thinking skills such as the ability to compare and contrast authors' credibility, facts, argumentation styles, use of persuasive techniques, and other stylistic tools. In short, the Opposing Viewpoints Series is an ideal way to attain the higher-level thinking and reading skills so essential in a culture of diverse and contradictory opinions.

In addition to providing a tool for critical thinking, Opposing Viewpoints books challenge readers to question their own strongly held opinions and assumptions. Most people form their opinions on the basis of upbringing, peer pressure, and personal, cultural, or professional bias. By reading carefully balanced opposing views, readers must directly confront new ideas as well as the opinions of those with whom they disagree. This is not to simplistically argue that everyone who reads opposing views will—or should—change his or her opinion. Instead, the series enhances readers' understanding of their own views by encouraging confrontation with opposing ideas. Careful examination of others' views can lead to the readers' understanding of the logical inconsistencies in their own opinions, perspective on why they hold an opinion, and the consideration of the possibility that their opinion requires further evaluation.

Evaluating Other Opinions

To ensure that this type of examination occurs, Opposing Viewpoints books present all types of opinions. Prominent spokespeople on different sides of each issue as well as well-known professionals from many disciplines challenge the reader. An additional goal of the series is to provide a forum for other, less known, or even unpopular viewpoints. The opinion of an ordinary person who has had to make the decision to cut off life support from a terminally ill relative, for example, may be just as valuable and provide just as much insight as a medical ethicist's professional opinion. The editors have two additional purposes in including these less known views. One, the editors encourage readers to respect others' opinions—even when not enhanced by professional credibility. It is only by reading or listening to and objectively evaluating others' ideas that one can determine whether they are worthy of consideration. Two, the inclusion of such viewpoints encourages the important critical thinking skill of objectively evaluating an author's credentials and bias. This evaluation will illuminate an author's reasons for taking a particular stance on an issue and will aid in readers' evaluation of the author's ideas.

It is our hope that these books will give readers a deeper understanding of the issues debated and an appreciation of the complexity of even seemingly simple issues when good and honest people disagree. This awareness is particularly important in a democratic society such as ours in which people enter into public debate to determine the common good. Those with whom one disagrees should not be regarded as enemies but rather as people whose views deserve careful examination and may shed light on one's own.

Thomas Jefferson once said that "difference of opinion leads to inquiry, and inquiry to truth." Jefferson, a broadly educated man, argued that "if a nation expects to be ignorant and free ... it expects what never was and never will be." As individuals and as a nation, it is imperative that we consider the opinions of others and examine them with skill and discernment. The Opposing Viewpoints Series is intended to help readers achieve this goal.

David L. Bender and Bruno Leone,
Founders

Introduction

"Few Americans realize that their cars can tattle on them. But among those in the know—civil libertarians, law enforcement agents and consumer advocates—a debate is surging. . . . While some welcome [event data recorders] as a safety measure, others fear them as an Orwellian intrusion." Margot Roosevelt, Time *magazine.*

About thirty-eight thousand people die each year as the result of an auto accident. The highest mortality rate occurs among otherwise healthy teens and young adults. These sad statistics have prompted many to consider auto accidents one of the most serious public health concerns in America. While efforts to improve auto safety and reduce the impact of auto accidents have had some success, policy makers continue to propose new strategies to further reduce the death toll. Some of these efforts generate rigorous debate. While few dispute the importance of improving public safety, some urge caution when these laws and policies threaten civil liberties. Indeed, one of the overarching themes that frame many controversies in the transportation policy debate is how to protect safety and security without trampling on individual liberties.

One controversy that reflects this recurrent theme concerns the popularly named "black box" that is installed in more than half of all new cars sold in the United States. The technical name for these devices is "event data recorder," or EDR. These devices collect information from a vehicle immediately before and during a serious "event" such as a collision. If there is in fact a crash, the EDR moves the last several seconds of information it has gathered to long-term storage.

General Motors (GM) installed the first EDR in 1974 to help deploy the air bags of its cars. By 1994, however, GM began installing much more sophisticated EDRs. The data captured varies among the auto manufacturers. Some record vehicle speed and data about air bag deployment alone. Others record whether the driver braked, used turn signals, or was wearing a seat belt. The uses of EDR data have also grown. EDRs were originally designed to provide information to help automakers build safer vehicles. However, police investigators and insurance companies soon saw the advantage of such information while investigating accidents and attempting to identify culpability. When people other than the automakers themselves began to request access to EDR data, the debate over its use began in earnest. While some see the EDR as a valuable tool to improve auto and road safety, others believe that without strict controls the device will violate civil liberties.

Safety experts, law enforcement, and insurance companies all tout the value of EDRs. "From a research point of view, there is absolutely no question in my mind that [the data] will lead to safer air bags and cars," claims Clay Gabler, professor of mechanical engineering at Virginia Tech's Center for Injury Biomechanics. For many EDR advocates, the safety value of the devices is sufficient to warrant mandating their use in all new passenger vehicles. "The information EDRs can provide is critical in understanding how people are injured in crashes, especially as auto manufacturers incorporate more sophisticated technologies," argues Sarah Ferguson, senior vice president of the Insurance Institute for Highway Safety (IIHS). "If EDRs were standard equipment," she maintains, "researchers as well as the automakers themselves would have a wider pool of reliable data to help evaluate occupant protection technology and answer other crashworthiness questions."

Proponents also see EDRs as a valuable legal tool. The devices have helped the families of victims obtain restitution against reckless drivers. One oft-cited example of the EDR's ability to identify culpability occurred following the deaths of a couple whose Jeep was struck by two teens racing down a suburban New York City street. One teen drove a new Mercedes, the other a two-year-old Corvette. Within a second of each other, the two cars, racing through an intersection, broadsided the couple's Jeep. One of the teens told a detective that the two teens were driving about 50 to 55 miles per hour. There was, however, another witness to the accident—the Corvette's EDR. The device revealed that the car had in fact been traveling 139 miles per hour. This information convinced a grand jury to indict the teens on murder charges.

EDR opponents question the safety motive of manufacturers and insurance carriers. If safety were the primary object, libertarian analyst Jim Harper asks, why are car manufacturers not flaunting the EDR's safety benefits as they do other improvements? Harper believes that they do not do so because the EDR "is not a safety feature; it is a surveillance tool—and when drivers learn about it, they are none too happy." EDR critics claim that the amount, type, and use of data should be limited. "We have a surveillance monster growing in our midst," claims Barry Steinhardt of the American Civil Liberties Union. "These black boxes are going to get more sophisticated and take on new capabilities," he warns.

California was the first state to address concerns about the EDR's impact on civil liberties. In 2004, California legislators passed a law that prohibits anyone from accessing EDR data without a car owner's permission or a subpoena. In Harper's view, however, this is a low level of privacy protection. "Consumers, not the government, should decide if they want their cars to collect such data, and if they want to share it with others." Federal agencies have also responded to the EDR controversy. In the spring of 2007, the National Highway Traffic Safety Administration (NHTSA) issued a new rule that establishes uniform standards for EDRs and that requires consumers be notified in the owner's manual that the vehicle is equipped with an EDR. U.S. auto manufacturers have until September 2010 to comply with these standards.

Advocates on both sides of the debate are dissatisfied with the NHTSA rules. Safety experts are disappointed that the administration did not require that EDRs be installed in all new cars. "The government should have gone further and mandated EDRs in all new passenger vehicles," claims IIHS's Ferguson. Privacy advocates, on the other hand, feel that the notice requirement is not strong enough to protect consumers. "Essentially what [NHTSA] has done is encourage more data collection without a corresponding increase or concern for privacy protection," claims Chris Hoofnagel, director of the Electronic Privacy Information Center.

Despite efforts to regulate EDRs, the debate remains heated. Whether the standards set by NHTSA are sufficient to improve traffic safety while at the same time adequately protecting consumer privacy remains to be seen. The authors of the viewpoints in *Opposing Viewpoints: Transportation* explore other issues concerning the nature and scope of transportation policy in the following chapters: What Alternative Transportation Strategies Are Best? What Transportation Policies Best Protect National Security? What Laws Best Protect Driver Safety? What Is the Future of Transportation?

What Alternative Transportation Strategies Are Best?

Chapter Preface

The personal transportation choice of a majority of Americans today is the automobile. During the last century, the automobile has increased personal freedom and mobility for many. However, Americans have become increasingly dependent on the automobile, and this dependence has created a variety of problems—traffic congestion, pollution, and the ever-increasing cost of maintaining roads and improving traffic safety. Current policy makers recommend a variety of strategies to reduce America's dependence on the automobile. One controversial strategy is to shift more transportation resources to the development of urban rail systems. Proponents maintain that urban rail systems are an excellent way to decrease energy consumption, improve the economic well-being of communities, and reduce pollution and traffic. Critics claim that the cost of such systems outweighs any benefits.

The primary reason proponents support increased investment in urban rail systems is that these systems reduce energy consumption. According to Todd Litman of the Victoria Transport Policy Institute, "Rail travel consumes about a fifth of the energy per passenger-mile as automobile travel." In fact, he asserts, "Each rail transit passenger-mile represents a reduction of 3 to 6 automobile vehicle-miles." Supporters also claim that urban rail systems provide a broad range of community benefits. "Rail transit and transit-oriented development can help improve community livability in several ways, including urban redevelopment, reduced vehicle traffic, reduced air and noise pollution, improved pedestrian facilities, and greater flexibility in parking requirements and street design," maintains Litman. Moreover, he reasons, "This provides direct benefits to residents, increases property values and can increase retail and tourist activity in an area."

Urban rail opponents contend that communities rarely realize the proposed benefits of these systems, and even when they do, the costs outweigh any potential benefits. Antirail advocate Randal O'Toole asserts, "The stampede to plan and build rail transit lines in American cities has led and is leading to a series of financial and mobility disasters." Libertarian analyst Ted Balaker agrees. "Light rail is expensive and ineffective—it almost always costs more to build and to operate than predicted," he maintains. Indeed, Balaker claims, "After spending billions on rail lines, after using aggressive zoning, and lavishing subsidies upon developers who pursue transit-oriented development, no light rail system has provided benefits anywhere near its costs." In fact, he argues, "Light rail does not account for even 1 percent of travel anywhere."

Whether urban rail systems are a bother or a benefit remains hotly contested. The authors in the following chapter present their views in answer to the question, What alternative transportation strategies are best?

> *"Ethanol is the most important and meaningful real world alternative we have to gasoline today."*

Ethanol Will Reduce America's Dependence on Crude Oil

Brian Jennings

American transportation depends on crude oil, much of which comes from other nations, claims Brian Jennings in the following viewpoint. Made from renewable resources by American farmers and local investors, ethanol can reduce this dependence, he argues. Jennings acknowledges that ethanol is not a magic bullet. Nevertheless, he reasons, global warming and a limited fuel supply suggest that ethanol should remain a vital part of America's progress toward energy independence. Jennings is executive vice president of the American Coalition for Ethanol, a grassroots organization dedicated to the production and use of ethanol.

As you read, consider the following questions:

1. According to Jennings, what fact about gasoline cannot be changed?

2. In the author's opinion, why do attacks on ethanol miss the mark?

Brian Jennings, "Ethanol: Breaking the Crude Oil Mandate," American Coalition for Ethanol, spring 2007. Reproduced by permission.

3. What government strategies does the author claim will ensure that the United States diversifies its energy supply?

Freedom, something we Americans celebrate proudly, means having the ability to make our own choices. But freedom quickly disappears when choices are not available. Having only one choice offers no real choice at all. Clearly this fact is lost upon ethanol critics who make hay from attacking ethanol.

A case in point about choices: the U.S. energy situation. Transportation fuel in America is almost completely sourced from crude oil—expensive crude oil that often comes from people and nations who don't like us very much. Gasoline can be marketed under different brands, grades, or octane levels, but the fact that it comes from a barrel of oil cannot change.

With no other choices but these petroleum-based fuels, we are essentially living under a de-facto crude oil mandate. Why have we independence-loving Americans put up with this status quo for so long? Ethanol, though just in its infancy, is beginning to break through this mandate and offer a real energy choice.

A Real World Alternative

Ethanol is not a silver bullet solution to America's energy situation, nor can it totally replace all the gasoline—140 billion gallons and growing—that the U.S. annually consumes. But ethanol is the most important and meaningful real world alternative we have to gasoline today, and it can diversify our transportation fuel supply, providing a domestically produced, cost-effective option at the pump.

Corn-based ethanol, much of it produced at facilities owned by farmers and local investors, has pioneered a place in the U.S. fuel supply, now being blended into nearly half of America's gasoline gallons. The 120 ethanol biorefineries across

How Does Ethanol Work?

Ethanol is a very high octane fuel, replacing lead as an octane enhancer in gasoline.

Fuels that burn too quickly make the engine "knock". The higher the octane rating, the slower the fuel burns, and the less likely the engine will knock.

When ethanol is blended with gasoline, the octane rating of the petrol goes up by three full points, without using harmful additives.

Adding ethanol to gasoline "oxygenates" the fuel, adding oxygen to the fuel mixture so that it burns more completely and reduces polluting emissions such as carbon monoxide.

Keith Addison.
http://journeytoforever.org/ethanol.html.

the nation have proven to be an important economic engine, restoring prosperity to rural communities and reducing farm program payouts due to the stronger domestic corn market.

Cellulosic ethanol will build upon the success that has already been accomplished, growing ethanol's footprint to a much larger portion of the fuel supply. By using a wide variety of cellulosic feedstocks—corn stover, grain straw, wood residues, municipal waste, citrus, perennial grasses—ethanol production can grow and so can the benefits to America's energy situation.

Yet it seems that everywhere you turn today, critics are questioning ethanol. They say government incentives and requirements are wrong. They say it takes too much fossil energy to create and transport ethanol. They say because ethanol is not a snap-your-fingers fix, it's not worthwhile.

The Energy Status Quo

These attacks are off the mark, and they detract from the real issue at hand: the energy status quo in this country is not working, and ethanol is part of the solution.

In the words of one petroleum company executive, asking the oil industry to sell ethanol is like asking cattlemen to sell tofu—it's not their product and they'd rather not use it. The transportation fuel supply is a pretty profitable status quo for the petroleum industry, and understandably, they have no reason to want things to change.

But as Americans, we do want things to change and understand that things must change. The threat of global warming and the reality of a limited oil supply are two red flags on the horizon, reminding us that clean, renewable alternatives are needed.

Congress is right to provide an incentive for ethanol, in the form of a lower fuel tax rate, as a way to encourage its inclusion in the gasoline supply. The Renewable Fuels Standard, requiring an increasing amount of ethanol and biodiesel to be used nationwide each year, is also a way to ensure that the U.S. moves forward into a diversified energy supply instead of remaining stuck in the oil status quo. Incentives are the government's way of supporting what it places value on, and in today's world, renewable fuels are undoubtedly worthy of efforts to help get them off the ground.

Ethanol has truly been a success story. A clean burning fuel made from renewable sources. A domestically produced fuel that adds value to chronically under-priced ag [agriculture] products and provides economic opportunity. A high quality, high octane fuel that adds to America's energy supply. We look forward to ethanol's continued and increasing success as a vehicle to move America toward energy independence.

> *"The case for ethanol is based on a baker's dozen myths."*

The Claimed Benefits of Ethanol Are Unfounded

John Stossel

Most of the claimed benefits of ethanol as an alternative fuel are untrue, argues John Stossel in the following viewpoint. Ethanol will not reduce U.S. dependence on foreign oil, he claims, because ethanol will meet only 12 percent of the demand for gasoline. Moreover, Stossel maintains, ethanol production uses as much energy as it produces and does not cut down on pollution. The only people who benefit from ethanol are corn farmers and those who process ethanol, he asserts. Stossel is a news correspondent and author of Myths, Lies, and Downright Stupidity: Get Out the Shovel—Why Everything You Know Is Wrong.

As you read, consider the following questions:

1. In Stossel's opinion, why does ethanol need government subsidies?
2. What will be the result of increased corn growing, in the author's view?

John Stossel, "The Many Myths of Ethanol," Townhall.com, March 23, 2007. Reproduced by permission of John Stossel and Creators Syndicate, Inc.

3. According to the author, why is ethanol a good issue for vote-hungry presidential hopefuls?

No doubt about it, if there were a Miss Energy Pageant, Miss Ethanol would win hands down. Everyone loves ethanol.

"Ramp up the availability of ethanol," says [2008 Democratic presidential contender] Hillary Clinton.

"Ethanol makes a lot of sense," says [2008 Republican presidential candidate] John McCain.

"The economics of ethanol make more and more sense," says [2008 Republican presidential contender] Mitt Romney.

"We've got to get serious about ethanol," says [2008 Republican presidential contender] Rudolph Giuliani.

And the media love ethanol. [TV newsmagazine] "60 Minutes" called it "the solution."

[Presidential candidates] Clinton, Romney, Barack Obama and John Edwards not only believe ethanol is the elixir that will give us cheap energy, end our dependence on Middle East oil sheiks, and reverse global warming, they also want you and me—as taxpayers—to subsidize it.

The Myths of Ethanol

When everyone in politics jumps on a bandwagon like ethanol, I start to wonder if there's something wrong with it. And there is. Except for the fact that ethanol comes from corn, nothing you're told about it is true. As the Cato Institute's energy expert Jerry Taylor said on a . . . "Myths" edition of [TV newsmagazine] "20/20," the case for ethanol is based on a baker's dozen myths.

A simple question first. If ethanol's so good, why does it need government subsidies? Shouldn't producers be eager to make it, knowing that thrilled consumers will reward them with profits?

But consumers won't reward them, because without subsidies, ethanol would cost much more than gasoline.

The claim that using ethanol will save energy is another myth. Studies show that the amount of energy ethanol produces and the amount needed to make it are roughly the same. "It takes a lot of fossil fuels to make the fertilizer, to run the tractor, to build the silo, to get that corn to a processing plant, to run the processing plant," Taylor says.

And because ethanol degrades, it can't be moved in pipelines the way that gasoline is. So many more big, polluting trucks will be needed to haul it.

More bad news: The increased push for ethanol has already led to a sharp increase in corn growing—which means much more land must be plowed. That means much more fertilizer, more water used on farms and more pesticides.

This makes ethanol the "solution"?

An Inadequate Solution

But won't it at least get us unhooked from Middle East oil? Wouldn't that be worth the other costs? Another myth. A University of Minnesota study shows that even turning all of America's corn into ethanol would meet only 12 percent of our gasoline demand. As Taylor told an energy conference, "For corn ethanol to completely displace gasoline consumption in this country, we would need to appropriate all cropland in the United States, turn it completely over to corn-ethanol production, and then find 20 percent more land on top of that for cultivation."

OK, but it will cut down on air pollution, right? Wrong again. Studies indicate that the standard mixture of 90 percent ethanol and 10 percent gasoline pollutes worse than gasoline.

Well, then, the ethanol champs must be right when they say it will reduce greenhouse gases and reverse global warming.

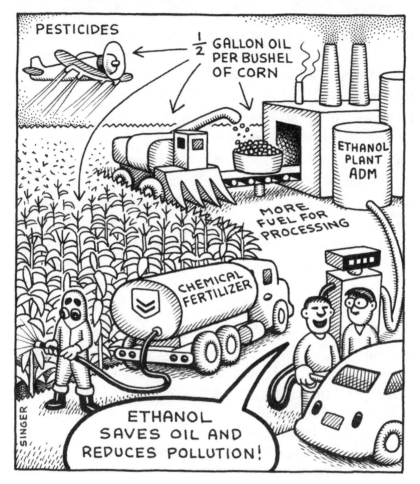

Nope. "Virtually all studies show that the greenhouse gases associated with ethanol are about the same as those associated with conventional gasoline once we examine the entire life cycle of the two fuels," Taylor says.

Surely, ethanol must be good for something. And here we finally have a fact. It *is* good for something—or at least someone: corn farmers and processors of ethanol, such as Archer

Daniels Midland, the big food processor known for its savvy at getting subsidies out of the taxpayers.

And it's good for vote-hungry presidential hopefuls. Iowa is a key state in the presidential-nomination sweepstakes, and we all know what they grow In Iowa. Sen. Clinton voted against ethanol 17 times until she started running for president. Coincidence?

"It's no mystery that people who want to be president support the corn ethanol program," Taylor says. "If you're not willing to sacrifice children to the corn god, you will not get out of the Iowa primary with more than one percent of the vote. Right now the closest thing we have to a state religion in the United States isn't Christianity. It's corn."

> "Hydrogen clearly provides the potential for huge energy and environmental improvements."

Hydrogen Has Significant Promise as an Alternative Fuel

Daniel Sperling and Joan Ogden

Hydrogen has enormous potential as a long-range solution to America's energy and environmental concerns, claim Daniel Sperling and Joan Ogden in the following viewpoint. While other alternative strategies provide short-term solutions, only hydrogen presents long-term benefits that will reduce pollution and U.S. dependence on foreign oil, the authors assert. Indeed, they argue, while oil companies and automakers have opposed other alternative fuels, they support the hydrogen alternative because they will maintain a role in the hydrogen economy. Sperling is a professor and director of the Institute of Transportation Studies at the University of California at Davis. Ogden is an associate professor at the University of California at Davis.

As you read, consider the following questions:

1. According to Sperling and Ogden, why is the history of alternative transportation a history of failures?

Daniel Sperling and Joan Ogden, "The Hope for Hydrogen," *Issues in Science & Technology*, spring 2004. Reproduced by permission.

2. In the authors' opinion, to what is the future of hydrogen linked?

3. What do the authors assert are the two "ifs" that must be resolved for hydrogen fuel cells to become a superior consumer automobile product?

The history of alternative transportation fuels is largely a history of failures. Methanol never progressed beyond its use in test fleets, despite support from President George H. W. Bush. Compressed natural gas remains a niche fuel. And nearly every major automotive company in the world has abandoned battery-electric vehicles. Only ethanol made from corn is gaining market share in the United States, largely because of federal and state subsidies and a federal mandate. Some alternatives have succeeded elsewhere for limited times, but always because of substantial subsidies and/or government protection.

Is hydrogen different? Why do senior executives of Shell, BP [British Petroleum], General Motors, Toyota, Daimler-Chrysler, Ford, and Honda tout hydrogen, and why do Presidents George [W.] Bush and Romano Prodi of the European Union and California Governor Arnold Schwarzenegger all advocate major hydrogen initiatives? Might hydrogen succeed on a grand scale, where other alternative fuels have not?

The Sources of Skepticism

Hydrogen clearly provides the potential for huge energy and environmental improvements. But skeptics abound, for many good reasons. Academics question near-term environmental benefits, and activists and environmental groups question the social, environmental, and political implications of what they call "black" hydrogen (because it would be produced from coal and nuclear power). Others say we are picking the wrong horse. Paul MacCready argues in the book of essays *The Hydrogen Energy Transition* that improved battery technology will trump hydrogen and fuel cell vehicles. And many, including John DeCicco of Environmental Defense, also in *The Hydrogen Energy Transition*, argue that the hydrogen transition is premature at best. A February 2004 report on hydrogen by the National Academies' National Academy of Engineering and National Research Council agrees, asserting that there are many questions to answer and many barriers to overcome before hydrogen's potential can be realized.

What is remarkable in the early stages of the debate is the source of public opposition: It is not coming from car or oil companies but primarily from those most concerned about environmental and energy threats. The core concern, as Joseph J. Romm argues so well . . . is that, "a major effort to introduce hydrogen cars before 2030 would actually undermine efforts to reduce emissions of heat-trapping greenhouse gases such as CO_2 [carbon dioxide]." . . .

We believe there is a different story to tell. First, hydrogen must be pursued as part of a long-term strategy. (Indeed, any coherent energy strategy should have a long-term component.) Second, hydrogen policy must complement and build on near-term policies aimed at energy efficiency, greenhouse gas reduction, and enhanced renewable energy investments. Hydrogen vehicles will not happen without those policies in place. In fact, hybrid vehicles are an essential step in the technological transition to fuel cells and hydrogen. And third, if not hydrogen, then what? No other long-term option approaches the breadth and magnitude of hydrogen's public benefits. . . .

The Case for Hydrogen

The case for hydrogen is threefold. First, hydrogen fuel cell vehicles appear to be a superior consumer product desired by the automotive industry. Second, as indicated by the National Academies' study, the potential exists for dramatic reductions in the cost of hydrogen production, distribution, and use. And third, hydrogen provides the potential for zero tailpipe pollution, near-zero well-to-wheels emissions of greenhouse gases, and the elimination of oil imports, simultaneously addressing the most vexing challenges facing the fuels sector, well beyond what could be achieved with hybrid vehicles and energy efficiency.

The future of hydrogen is linked to the automotive industry's embrace of fuel cells. The industry, or at least an important slice of it, sees fuel cells as its inevitable and desired future. This was not true for any previous alternative fuel. The National Academies' report highlights the attractions of fuel cell vehicles. It notes that not only are fuel cells superior environmentally, but they also provide extra value to customers. They have the potential to provide most of the benefits of battery-electric vehicles without the short range and long recharge time. They offer quiet operation, rapid acceleration from a standstill because of the torque characteristics of electric motors, and potentially low maintenance requirements. They can provide remote electrical power—for construction sites and recreational uses, for example—and even act as distributed electricity generators when parked at homes and offices. Importantly, they also have additional attractions for automakers. By eliminating most mechanical and hydraulic subsystems, they provide greater design flexibility and the potential for using fewer vehicle platforms, which allow more efficient manufacturing approaches. Fuel cells are a logical extension of the technological pathway automakers are already following and would allow a superior consumer product—if fuel cell costs become competitive and if hydrogen fuel can be made widely available at a reasonable cost.

Resolving the "Ifs"

Those two "ifs" remain unresolved and are central to the hydrogen debate. Fuel cell costs are on a steep downward slope and are now perhaps a factor of 10 to 20 too high. Huge amounts of engineering are still needed to improve manufacturability, ensure long life and reliability, and enable operation at extreme temperatures. Although some engineers believe that entirely new fuel cell architectures are needed to achieve the last 10-fold cost reduction, a handful of automotive companies seem convinced that they are on track to achieve those necessary cost reductions and performance enhancements. Indeed, massive R&D [research and development] investments are taking place at most of the major automakers.

The second "if" is hydrogen availability, which is perhaps the greatest challenge of all. The problem is not production cost or sufficient resources. Hydrogen is already produced from natural gas and petroleum at costs similar to those of gasoline (adjusting for fuel cells' higher efficiency). With continuing R&D investment, the cost of providing hydrogen from a variety of abundant fossil and renewable sources should prove to be not much greater than that of providing gasoline, according to the National Academies' study.

The key supply challenges are as follows. First is the need for flexibility. There are many possible paths for making and delivering hydrogen, and it is difficult at this time to know which will prevail. Second, because private investment will naturally gravitate toward conventional fossil energy sources, currently the lowest-cost way to make hydrogen, government needs to accelerate R&D of zero-emission hydrogen production methods. Renewable hydrogen production is a key area for focused R&D. CO_2 sequestration—a prerequisite if abundant coal in the United States, China, and elsewhere is to be used—is another possible path to very-low-emission hydrogen. Although the cost of capturing carbon from large fossil fuel plants and sequestering it is not prohibitive in a large range of locations and situations, CO_2 sequestration faces uncertain public acceptance. Will CO_2 be perceived in the same light as nuclear waste, leading to permitting delays and extra costs?

Developing Distribution Systems

The third supply-related challenge is logistical in nature. How can hydrogen be provided at local refueling sites, offering both convenience and acceptable cost to consumers during a transition? Today's natural gas and petroleum distribution systems are not necessarily good models for future hydrogen distribution, especially in the early stages of hydrogen use when consumption is small and dispersed. If future hydrogen systems attempt to simply mimic today's energy systems from the beginning, distribution costs could be untenably large, and the hydrogen economy will be stillborn. Unlike liquid transportation fuels, hydrogen storage, delivery, and refueling are major cost contributors. Astoundingly, delivering hydrogen from large plants to dispersed small hydrogen users is now roughly five times more expensive than producing the hydrogen. Even for major fossil fuel–based hydrogen production facilities under study, distribution and delivery costs are estimated to be equal to production costs.

Clearly, a creative, evolutionary approach is needed, eventually leading to a system that serves both stationary and mobile users, relies on small as well as large hydrogen production facilities, accesses a wide variety of energy feedstocks, incorporates CO_2 capture and sequestration, and is geographically diverse. In the very early stages of a transition, hydrogen might be delivered by truck from a central plant serving chemical uses as well as vehicles or be produced at refueling sites from natural gas or electricity. Distributed generation will be a key part of the solution, with production near or at the end-use site. The National Academies' report argues that the hydrogen economy will initially and perhaps for a very long time be based on distributed generation of hydrogen. (Honda and General Motors propose placing small hydrogen refueling appliances at residences.) Other innovative solutions would be needed, especially during the early phases. In cities with dense populations, pipelines would probably become the lowest-cost delivery option, once a sizeable fraction of vehicles run on hydrogen. The transportation fuel and electricity and chemical industries might become more closely coupled, because the economics can sometimes be improved by coproduction of electricity, hydrogen, and chemical products. Transitions would proceed in different ways, depending on regional resources and geographic factors.

No Natural Enemies

Although the challenges are daunting, perhaps the most important factor is the absence of natural political or economic enemies. For starters, hydrogen is highly inclusive, capable of being made from virtually any energy feedstock, including coal, nuclear, natural gas, biomass, wind, and solar.

The oil industry is key. It effectively opposed battery-electric vehicles, because companies saw no business case for themselves. Hydrogen is different. Oil companies are in actuality massive energy companies. They are prepared to supply any liquid or gaseous fuel consumers might desire, although of course they prefer a slow transition that allows them to protect their current investments. Most, for instance, prefer that initial fuel cell vehicles carry reformers to convert gasoline into hydrogen. They have been disappointed that all major car companies are now focused strictly on delivered hydrogen.

Oil companies will not allow the hydrogen economy to develop without them. Indeed, some have played key roles in promoting hydrogen, and many are active participants in hydrogen-refueling demonstration projects around the world. But oil companies would not realize a rapid payoff from being the first to market. Rather, they anticipate large financial losses that would be stanched only when hydrogen use became widespread. Without government support during the low-volume transition stage, oil companies are unlikely to be early investors in the construction of hydrogen fuel stations. They are best characterized as watchful, strategically positioning themselves to play a large role if and when hydrogen takes off.

Automakers see a different business reality. They see benefits from being first to market. They see hydrogen fuel cells as the desirable next step in the technological evolution of vehicles. Hydrogen's future appears to be tightly linked to automaker commitments to move fuel cells from the lab to the marketplace. The key question is whether and when they will ratchet up current investments of perhaps $150 million per year (in the case of the more aggressive automakers) to the much larger sums needed to tool factories and launch commercial products. Without automaker leadership, the transition will be slow, building on small entrepreneurial investments in niche opportunities, such as fuel cells in off-road industrial equipment, hydrogen blends in natural gas buses, innovative low-cost delivery of hydrogen to small users, and small energy stations simultaneously powering remote buildings and vehicle fleets.

If Not Hydrogen, What?

What are the alternatives to hydrogen? The only other serious long-term alternatives for fueling the transport sector are grid-supplied electricity and biomass. Electricity is quite appealing on environmental and energy grounds. It allows for many of the same benefits as hydrogen: accessing renewable and other feedstocks and zero vehicular emissions. But every major automaker has abandoned its battery-electric vehicle program, except for DaimlerChrysler's small factory in North Dakota producing the GEM neighborhood vehicle. For battery-electric vehicles to be viable, several-fold improvements in batteries or other electricity storage devices would be required, or massive investments would be needed in "third rail" electricity infrastructure that would require substantial added cost for vehicles. These massive improvements are unlikely. Continued battery improvements are likely, but after a

How Hydrogen Fuel Cells Work

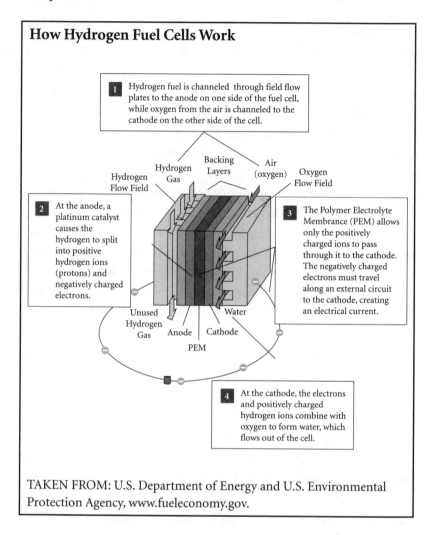

1 Hydrogen fuel is channeled through field flow plates to the anode on one side of the fuel cell, while oxygen from the air is channeled to the cathode on the other side of the cell.

Hydrogen Flow Field
Hydrogen Gas
Backing Layers
Air (oxygen)
Oxygen Flow Field

2 At the anode, a platinum catalyst causes the hydrogen to split into positive hydrogen ions (protons) and negatively charged electrons.

3 The Polymer Electrolyte Membrane (PEM) allows only the positively charged ions to pass through it to the cathode. The negatively charged electrons must travel along an external circuit to the cathode, creating an electrical current.

Unused Hydrogen Gas
Anode
Cathode
Water
PEM

4 At the cathode, the electrons and positively charged hydrogen ions combine with oxygen to form water, which flows out of the cell.

TAKEN FROM: U.S. Department of Energy and U.S. Environmental Protection Agency, www.fueleconomy.gov.

century of intense research, there still remains no compelling proposal that might reduce material costs sufficiently to render batteries competitive with internal combustion engines. The same is not true of fuel cells.

The other long-term proposal is biomass. Cellulosic materials, including trees and grasses, would be grown on the vast land areas of the United States and converted into ethanol or methanol fuel for use in combustion engines. Although this energy option is renewable, the environmental effects of intensive farming are not trivial, and the land areas involved are massive. Moreover, there are few other regions in the world available for extensive energy farming.

Other options include fossil-based synthetic fuels, in which shale oil, oil sands, coal, and other abundant materials are converted into petroleum-like fuels and then burned in combustion engines or converted into hydrogen at fuel stations or on board vehicles for use in fuel cells. But with all these options, carbon capture at the site is more difficult than with coal-to-hydrogen options, CO_2 volumes would be massive, and the overall energy efficiency would be far inferior.

We conclude that hydrogen merits strong support, if only because of the absence of a more compelling long-term option.

Hydrogen's Precarious Future

The transition to a hydrogen economy will be neither easy nor straightforward. Like all previous alternatives, it faces daunting challenges. But hydrogen is different. It accesses a broad array of energy resources, potentially provides broader and deeper societal benefits than any other option, potentially provides large private benefits, has no natural political or economic enemies, and has a strong industrial proponent in the automotive industry.

In the end, though, the hydrogen situation is precarious. Beyond a few car companies and a scattering of entrepreneurs, academics, and environmental advocates, support for hydrogen is thin. Although many rail against the hydrogen hype, the greater concern perhaps should be the fragile support for hydrogen. Politics aside, we applaud the United States, California, and others for starting down a path toward a sustainable future. Although we do not know when or even if the hydrogen economy will eventually dominate, we do believe that starting down this path is good strategy.

The key is enhanced science and technology investments, both public and private, and a policy environment that encourages those investments. Fuel cells and hydrogen provide a good marker to use in formulating policy and gaining public support. Of course, policy should remain focused on near-term opportunities. But good near-term policy, such as improving fuel economy, is also good long-term policy. It sends signals to businesses and customers that guide them toward investments and market decisions that are beneficial to society. It appears to us that hydrogen is a highly promising option that we should nurture as part of a broader science, technology, and policy initiative. The question is how, not if.

| "Numerous studies of a hydrogen economy rely on assumptions that are overly optimistic."

The Promise of Hydrogen as an Alternative Fuel Is Exaggerated

Joseph J. Romm

Claims about the promise of hydrogen are more hype than hope, argues Joseph J. Romm in the following viewpoint. The costs of producing hydrogen from renewable energy sources are substantial and producing hydrogen from fossil fuels creates greenhouse gases, he maintains. Transportation systems based on hydrogen will be much slower in coming than advocates claim, Romm asserts. Unfortunately, he reasons, creating unrealistic expectations about hydrogen threatens its long-term potential. Romm is a fellow at the Center for American Progress and author of The Hype About Hydrogen: Fact and Fiction in the Race to Save the Climate, *from which the following viewpoint is taken.*

As you read, consider the following questions:

1. According to Romm, on what two pillars does the hydrogen economy rest?

Joseph J. Romm, from, *The Hype About Hydrogen: Fact and Fiction in the Race to Save the Climate*. Island Press, 2004. Reproduced by permission.

2. In the author's opinion, what impact does the threat of global warming from greenhouse gases have on the production of hydrogen for cars?

3. In the author's view, why are conservative assumptions about the hydrogen economy essential?

Imagine a world in which you can drive your car to work each day without consuming any oil or producing any pollution. When you park your car at work or at home, you hook it up to the power grid, generating pollution-free electricity for your community. And, as part of the deal, you get money back from your utility.

You are living in the hydrogen economy, a high-tech Eden. Is it too good to be true? Will it happen in your lifetime?

The Fuel Cell

The environmental paradise of a hydrogen economy rests on two pillars: a pollution-free source for the hydrogen itself and a device for converting it into useful energy without generating pollution. Let's start with the fuel cell—a small, modular electrochemical device, similar to a battery, but which can be continuously fueled. For most purposes, think of a fuel cell as a black box that takes in hydrogen and oxygen and puts out water plus electricity and heat, but no pollution whatsoever.

The first commercial stationary fuel cell was introduced in the early 1990s by United Technologies Corporation. Since fuel cells have no moving parts, they hold the promise of high reliability, and since power outages had caused countless business disruptions in the late 1990s, the product seemed like a sure winner.

These fuel cells were first used to provide guaranteed ultra-reliable power in the Technology Center of the First National Bank of Omaha. The center processes credit card orders from all over the country. "A single major retail client can lose as much as $6 million an hour if the Center's power fails and orders are not processed," reported Thomas Ditoro, the project's electrical engineer. In the bank's previous facility, its customers had experienced substantial losses from a power outage and failure of a battery backup system. That is why the First National Bank installed the most reliable electric power source it could find, a system developed by SurePower Corporation combining fuel cells with other advanced energy and electronic devices.

The bank needed to maximize the availability of its computer system to protect existing clients while attracting new ones. A traditional system, combining an uninterruptible power supply (UPS) with power from the electric grid and backup diesel generators, would have more than a 63 percent probability of a major failure over its 20-year life. The Sure-Power system has less than a 1 percent chance of a major failure in 20 years. This may well be the difference between business success or bankruptcy.

After the system was installed in mid-1999, the bank used its new ultra-reliable power as a key feature in its marketing campaign, and as a result it has increased its market share. Dennis Hughes, the bank's lead property manager, said that the system's high reliability "isn't a luxury for us" but rather is a "competitive advantage. With SurePower, First National can raise our customers' service expectations while generating higher revenues." Although the initial cost of the fuel cell system was higher than that of the traditional UPS system, the life-cycle costs were much lower—a winning choice in every way.

I started working with SurePower during this project and performed an environmental analysis of the system. I found many benefits other than high reliability and low life-cycle cost. Compared with a traditional system using a UPS and the electric grid, the SurePower system had a superior environmental performance. It had more than 40 percent lower emissions of carbon dioxide (CO_2, the primary greenhouse gas) and less than one one-thousandth the emissions of other air pollutants. Intrigued, I became an investor in the company, and later I helped it make an advance sale of the greenhouse gas credits that would be created by its next pollution-reducing project.

The Challenges of the Hydrogen Economy

And yet *for more than four years after* its highly successful First National Bank of Omaha project, SurePower still was not able to sell a second high-reliability system to any other customer. Moreover, the manufacturer of the fuel cells themselves, UTC Fuel Cells, had only limited success selling the product for other applications and is phasing them out to pursue a different fuel cell technology. Exploring the complicated reasons for this unexpected business outcome will help explain the challenges to, as well as the benefits of, accelerating the commercialization of stationary fuel cells.

Assuming we succeed with fuel cells, we must still find affordable, pollution-free sources for hydrogen to achieve a true hydrogen economy. We are a long way from finding them. The person credited with originating the phrase "hydrogen economy" in the early 1970s, Australian electrochemist John Bockris, wrote in 2002, "Boiled down to its minimalist description, the 'Hydrogen Economy' means that hydrogen would be used to transport energy from renewables (at nuclear or solar sources) over large distances; and to store it (for supply to cities) in large amounts." Our cars, our homes, our industries would be powered not by pollution-generating fossil fuels—coal, gas, and oil, much of which is imported from geopolitically unstable regions—but by hydrogen from pollution-free domestic sources.

Unfortunately, the costs of producing hydrogen from renewable energy sources are extraordinarily high and likely to remain so for decades, given current U.S. energy policies. Virtually all hydrogen today is produced from fossil fuels in processes that generate significant quantities of greenhouse gases. Although a number of people have characterized the hydrogen economy as being just around the corner, what they are actually promoting is an economy built around hydrogen made from natural gas and other polluting fossil fuels.

Running *stationary* fuel cells on hydrogen produced from natural gas makes a great deal of sense and seems likely in the near future. But a transportation system based on hydrogen will be much slower in coming and more difficult to achieve than is widely appreciated. The technological challenges are immense. More important, *fueling cars with hydrogen made from natural gas makes no sense, either economically or environmentally.* The rapidly growing threat of global warming demands that hydrogen for cars be produced from sources that do not generate greenhouse gases. . . .

A Realistic View

Many clean energy companies were overhyped in the late 1990s, in part because of a strange myth that, because the internet and related information technology equipment supposedly consumed a great deal of electricity, the rapid growth in the internet would lead to rapid growth in electricity demand. This, it was argued, would benefit all technologies that provide electricity but especially those that could provide reliable power, such as fuel cells. Several major brokerage firms released their own "analyses" repeating this myth and touting a variety of energy technology stocks. The myth was utterly refuted by the Lawrence Berkeley National Laboratory, the Rand Corporation, and my own Center for Energy and Climate Solutions, among others: The internet is not, in fact, a big electricity draw, and its growth has little, if any, effect on overall growth in electricity demand.

The near-term prospects for fuel cell vehicles were also overhyped in the late 1990s. In November 2002, a major study titled "Hybrid & Competitive Automobile Powerplants" con-

The Real Challenge

Amidst the hydrogen hype, few have noted where the new fuel comes from: fossil fuels. As it stands, burning hydrogen reduces neither demand for fossil fuels nor emissions of carbon dioxide, because almost all the hydrogen used today comes from natural gas.

Matthew S. Meisel, Harvard Crimson, *September 20, 2006.*

cluded, "The industry is currently experiencing a backlash to the 'just around the corner' hype that has surrounded the automotive fuel cell in recent years."

Not surprisingly, from fuel cells to microturbines, many stocks that soared in the NASDAQ boom plummeted in the bust. For instance, the company that assumed a leadership role in transportation fuel cells in the 1980s and 1990s, the company with the most patents and the most major deals with automakers, is Ballard Power Systems Inc. This Canadian company was even the subject of a very favorable 1999 book, *Powering the Future,* in which executives were quoted as assuring profitability within a year or two. The stock price soared in the late 1990s. By December 2002, the price had dropped back to 1997 levels. The company announced that it was laying off 400 people, one-quarter of the workforce, and did not expect to achieve profitability for five years. And yet Ballard remains one of the leaders in fuel cells. Commercializing new energy technologies is much harder than is widely realized.

The Lessons of the Marketplace

For a number of years, I have divided my time between working with small companies trying to market the next breakthrough technology and helping Fortune 500 companies design strategies to cut energy costs and reduce greenhouse gas emissions. This work, together with my earlier time at the U.S. Department of Energy, has taught me two large lessons about the marketplace.

First, most companies are very conservative about purchasing and deploying new technology. A small number of firms are aggressive first adopters, but the vast majority buy only products that have both a good commercial track record and a very rapid payback. Even many brand-named companies will invest only in an energy technology that pays for itself in energy savings within about a year.

Second, those in the public or private sector who advocate new technologies tend to overestimate how rapidly they will achieve their performance and cost goals while underestimating what the competition will do. Renewable energy still suffers from the marketplace perception that it has failed to deliver on promises made in the 1970s, although for more than a decade now both solar power and wind power have been growing rapidly, and most renewable energy technologies have met or exceeded their cost and performance goals. Nonetheless, renewable energy does not now provide a bigger share of U.S. energy mainly because the competition got tougher. Fossil fuel technologies in particular now have both reduced costs and reduced pollution.

Hydrogen faces a similar set of obstacles. Yet numerous studies of a hydrogen economy rely on assumptions that are overly optimistic. For instance, many analyses assume that the total delivered cost for hydrogen need be reduced only to a level at which it is twice that of gasoline (for an equivalent amount of energy delivered). The argument is made that hydrogen fuel cells are twice as efficient as gasoline internal combustion engines, so the fuel can be twice as expensive and consumers will still end up paying the same total fuel bill. But that is comparing a future technology with a current technology—and not even the best current technology. Hybrid gasoline-electric vehicles *today*, such as the Toyota Prius, are already much more efficient than traditional internal combustion engine vehicles and nearly as efficient as *projected* fuel cell vehicles (assuming fuel cells achieve their performance targets). A hybrid diesel-electric vehicle would have about the same overall efficiency as a fuel cell vehicle. That's tough competition for hydrogen.

Given the numerous large roadblocks that hydrogen fuel cell vehicles must overcome to become competitive products, and given the history of other advanced energy technologies, we should avoid both overly optimistic assumptions about new technologies and underestimation of the competition. Indeed, considering the tens of billions of dollars for infrastructure that the government (and hence U.S. taxpayers) will have to devote to bring about a hydrogen economy, conservative assumptions are essential. The energy and environmental problems facing the nation and the world, especially global warming, are far too serious to risk making major policy mistakes that misallocate scarce resources....

The Risk of Hype

I am very hopeful that the sunnier predictions will ultimately prove true, but our limited experience with commercializing fuel cells provides a multi-decade lesson in high-tech humility. And our recent experience in trying to accelerate the introduction of alternative fuel vehicles provides a lesson in how difficult it will be to rapidly change gasoline-powered cars and the gasoline infrastructure. One hard lesson learned is that overhyping new technologies ultimately ends up slowing their success in the market.

Unfortunately, the usual sources for good information have often been unreliable, a testimony to the enormous difficulty of analyzing the many factors involved in the transition to a pollution-free hydrogen economy. Most of the articles and books on the subject in recent years—including articles in such prestigious publications as *Technology Review, Wired* magazine, and the *Atlantic Monthly*—fail to distinguish between likely scenarios for the future and unlikely ones. They often contain serious errors and misleading statements.

Just as importantly, major corporations such as General Motors [GM] continue to overhype the near-term prospect for hydrogen cars. GM is wildly overestimating the speed of successful mass-market introduction of hydrogen cars, which it says will start around 2010, while underestimating the competition from hybrids. GM is spending a large fraction of its research budget on hydrogen-powered cars—which . . . is a strategic mistake. . . .

Hydrogen vehicles are unlikely to achieve even a 5 percent market penetration by 2030. And this in turn leads to the . . . major conclusion . . .: *Neither government policy nor business investment should be based on the belief that hydrogen cars will have meaningful commercial success in the near- or medium-term.*

> "[Public transit] offers increased travel
> choices through a redundant system not
> reliant solely on the automobile."

Public Transportation Will Reduce Urban Congestion

Lester Hoel

In cities big and small, too many vehicles in too little space has led to traffic congestion, a problem that cannot be resolved simply by building more highways, claims Lester Hoel in the following viewpoint. However, he maintains, integrated public transportation systems can conserve energy and space and strengthen city centers by connecting people from rural areas and those with limited mobility to the culture and opportunities available in cities. Public transportation has a significant impact on a city's economy and deserves public support. Hoel, professor of engineering at the University of Virginia, is coeditor of the textbook Public Transportation.

As you read, consider the following questions:

1. What does Hoel claim is the key challenge of urban transportation systems?

Lester Hoel, "Why Public Transit Deserves Our Support,"*Progressive Engineer*, February 2005. © 2004 Progressive Engineer. Reproduced by permission.

2. Why, in the author's view, did the railroad industry abandon much of its commuter rail service in the 1950s?

3. According to the author, why is public transit even more essential to urban health and welfare in the twenty-first century?

The strength of cities has been tied to transportation since the dawn of civilization. Whether a protected ocean harbor or the convergence of trade routes in the desert, physical access and the availability of transportation facilities have exerted a powerful influence on a city's economy, social fabric, and culture. Even today, cities and countries without good transportation systems are at an economic disadvantage.

The Problem of Congestion

The key challenge of urban transportation systems is congestion—too many vehicles and too little space. This phenomenon is not new: Julius Caesar had to deal with the problem; he banned wheeled traffic from the center of Rome.

Congestion is linked to several inescapable factors of modern life: urbanization, which concentrates people and activities; industrialization, which creates a separation and specialization of activities at home and work; and the difficulties arising from a constant supply of transportation infrastructure (roads and transit lines) serving a variable demand, the "peak hour," which leads to rush-hour traffic.

In the 20th century, there were urban transportation problems of crisis proportions. One of these was the railroad industry's abandonment of much of their commuter rail service in the 1950s as an unprofitable business. Although there was still considerable demand, America's growing love affair with cars and the freedom they promised was proving a formidable competitor. Later, with construction of the urban portions of the national interstate highway system, transit de-

Public Transportation Reduces Energy Consumption

Public transportation can significantly reduce our nation's dependency on gasoline. For every passenger mile traveled, public transportation uses about one half of the fuel consumed by cars, and about a third of that used by sport utility vehicles and light trucks.

Each year, public transportation use in the U.S. saves:

- 1.4 billion gallons of gasoline, representing 4 million gallons of gasoline per day

- The equivalent of 34 supertankers of oil, or a supertanker leaving the Middle East every 11 days

- The equivalent of 140,000 fewer service station tanker trucks clogging our streets each year

- The equivalent of 300,000 fewer automobile fillups each day.

American Public Transportation Association,
Public Transportation Fact Book, *2007.*

mand would lag even further. Big city mayors, fearful of the economic disruption, the added traffic burden, and the need to support a viable public transportation service, lobbied the federal government to support public transit in urban areas.

Recognizing transit as an essential city service that should not be held captive to the whims of the marketplace, the federal government in 1961 provided funds for capital investments in public transit. In 1967 the U.S. Department of Transportation and a key division, the Urban Mass Transit Administration, later renamed the Federal Transit Administration, were formed. Today, urban transportation is less crisis driven, yet constantly in the news. It ranks high among local concerns and often is a hot-button, political issue.

In suburbs, exurbs, and smaller cities, where the demand is less concentrated, highway gridlock has become a problem. But building more and bigger highways isn't always the answer, because such improvements may stimulate demand and add to the traffic. Most transportation planners agree that we can't build our way out of congestion.

Supporting Public Transit

Instead, cities need integrated transportation networks that bring together trains, buses, planes, automobiles, and perhaps ferries in a system that produces reliable, safe, and congestion-free travel. They need to provide transportation to residents who cannot drive automobiles, whether due to age, income, or health. Serving these groups provides a strong rationale for supporting public transit.

Other reasons include grappling with the regional environmental impact and land-use concerns relating to ever-expanding automobile use in the surrounding suburbs and exurbs. Urban planners are trying to incorporate stronger public transit systems into livable city designs, using principles of "smart growth" to keep cities attractive and accessible while providing thoughtful opportunities for transportation choices.

Public transit is even more vital to urban health and welfare in the 21st century. It offers increased travel choices through a redundant system not reliant solely on the automobile; mobility for all citizens, and special services for the elderly and handicapped; conservation of urban space devoted to transportation through reduced traffic congestion and limited need for parking space; and economic benefits to society from the reduced per-trip cost in many situations. City centers cannot survive without public transit, now or in the future.

Mass transit provides options responsive to local needs and the political process. It can strengthen the central core of large cities and serve as a backup system. It can conserve energy and space. In partnership with other modes of transportation, it can serve both urban and rural groups that would otherwise have diminished mobility and accessibility to city jobs and cultural life.

Public transit deserves our continued support!

> "*[People] seek the freedom of work choices and life opportunities that cars make possible.*"

Public Transportation Will Not Diminish Americans' Love of Cars

Joel Kotkin

Americans will continue to choose cars over public transportation because of the freedom of choice and opportunity that cars provide, asserts Joel Kotkin in the following viewpoint. When gas prices rise, he maintains, Americans do not shift to public transportation but adjust by buying thriftier cars. In fact, despite claims by advocates who romanticize traditional public transit, those who drive cars to work have shorter commutes than those who use public transportation, Kotkin claims. American mobility has and will continue to spur the nation's economic growth, he argues. Kotkin is a fellow at the New America Foundation, a centrist think tank.

Joel Kotkin, "Transit for the Public, Not the Planners," *American Enterprise*, vol. 17, June 2006, pp. 29–33. Copyright 2006 American Enterprise Institute for Public Policy Research. Reproduced with permission of *The American Enterprise*, a national magazine of Politics, Business, and Culture (TAEmag.com).

As you read, consider the following questions:

1. According to Kotkin, with what did America create the wealthiest society in human history?
2. In the author's opinion, of what were America's vast suburbs a product?
3. What, in the author's view, should the transportation goal of our nation be?

A merica is a society built on mobility. With bold sailing ships, intricate canals, ambitious railways, and brilliantly engineered highways and airports, we have created the wealthiest large society in human history, and done so while spending increasingly less of our wealth on getting around. At the height of the rail era, notes Harvard scholar Ed Glaeser, transportation accounted for 9 percent of GDP [gross domestic product], while today it represents 2 percent.

In this respect, our shift to ever more flexible and efficient engine-driven automobiles, trucks, and planes should be seen as a major technological feat. Yet instead of celebrating our successes, some policy, academic, and media elites are hectoring for a return to the centralized, rail-centric model of transit that prevailed in earlier centuries. Advocates speak approvingly of forcing American commuting patterns "back to the way we were." They romanticize the densely packed cities dependent on public transit that prevailed several generations ago. Their backward-looking agenda leaves them at war against cars, and against suburbs where most of us choose to live.

Mistaken Priorities

The views of these fashionable public transport "visionaries" have little to do with the realities of how average Americans raise families, travel, and work. Many of them appear to have about as much comprehension of the aspirations and needs of middle America as they do of Inner Mongolians.

Take, for example, the current push for "light rail" systems, even in such unlikely places as Boise, Idaho. In a society that is spreading out and deconcentrating, where work is detaching from centralized employment centers, where family life and leisure are more and more personalized and custom-cut, this makes little sense. Yet scores of cities have spent hundreds of millions of dollars to build such inflexible iron systems, and many more are considering doing so.

Such mistaken priorities threaten the future mobility of an amazingly vital society that by 2050 will add roughly one hundred million people. Already we have not built enough roads, which is why average travel times have increased from 22 to 26 minutes in recent decades. Although they still represent a small minority, workers commuting more than 45 minutes to their jobs have increased from 13 to 15 percent of the U.S. total. Road congestion clearly poses an economic threat as well, producing an estimated $520 in extra annual per capita costs in the nation's 75 largest metro areas. Travel blockages also erode the quality of community and family life.

Clearly, increased investment in mobility will be necessary to alleviate these problems. Some of this should involve flexible forms of public transit—like buses and private jitneys. Other innovations like toll roads—increasingly popular in Europe and elsewhere—will make car travel and truck transport alike more efficient and sensible. We also need to reduce the "demand" for travel by harnessing the computer and telecom revolutions to cut back commuting, and by creating more self-sustaining communities across the broad American landscape. This makes far more sense than the current fashion of trying to boost the density of existing hub-and-spoke cities.

But it's important we invest wisely in our future spending on transportation. The costs will be substantial, and misallocated resources could easily be wasted, or even counterproductive. Americans need to think boldly about our future

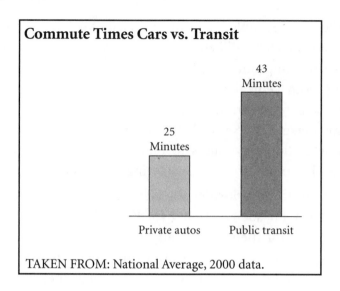

Commute Times Cars vs. Transit

43 Minutes

25 Minutes

Private autos   Public transit

TAKEN FROM: National Average, 2000 data.

transportation needs, and not just try to recreate the past, or coerce citizens into some preferred future. . . .

Cars Beat Trains, Period

The recent surge in energy prices, however, has given new vigor to the anti-auto, anti-suburban critics. "Let the Gloating Begin," they say, predicting a general catastrophe for the suburbs. Urban boosters are expressing renewed hope for a massive return to public transit and densely packed center cities.

However, earlier energy price surges—which were far steeper during the 1970s, for instance, than today—did not drive Americans back into cities or subway cars. People didn't react by moving into the city or jumping on mass transit in appreciable numbers; the 1970s were the one decade in the last century when overall urban population actually dropped. Rather, suburbanization proceeded apace, both demographically and economically. Americans adjusted to higher prices in other ways, like shifting to thriftier auto models. Car mileage improved from an average of 13 miles per gallon to 22.

Today, there again seems to be strengthened interest in fuel efficient cars. But driving itself (not to mention living patterns) will probably not change much over time. Even with a 24 percent jump in gas prices between 2004 and 2005, vehicle miles traveled in the U.S. basically remained unchanged, according to U.S. government data. America's homes and jobs have spread out massively over the last generation, and this will not change in the future. In fact, it is likely to accelerate.

Contrary to romantic conspiracy theories, it wasn't conniving oil companies, or road builders, or developers, or Madison Avenue sharks, or dullard traffic engineers who created the demand for the suburbs and put us in our cars. Instead, America's vast suburbs were a product of deep and very natural human longings—which in America even ordinary working-class citizens were suddenly in a position to fulfill, thanks to the nation's unprecedented economic success.

What People Want

Yes, people like walking districts and restored Main Streets and bike trails, but they also seek the freedom of work choices and life opportunities that cars make possible. They want to be able to pick up their kids, go to church, and shop when and where they choose. And they want to live in places that are quiet, safe, private, and peaceful—things that have never been common in center cities.

As a result, the long-term outlook for traditional public transit—no matter how much public money is spent on new light rail systems—is not particularly bright. Transit's share of the nation's total travel has continued to drop. One reason: transit riders are far more likely to suffer long commutes than those who drive. Contrary to media accounts, residents of suburbs and exurbs actually have the country's shortest commutes, while the areas with the longest average commutes— like New York and Chicago—are dense cities with extensive transit systems and centralized business districts. In contrast, places like Houston have far shorter average commutes.

But so much for logic. Cities large and small continue to fantasize about, and spend large sums on, new public transport systems that planners imagine will lure drivers out of their cars and revitalize inner cities. Unfortunately, experience shows that light rail lines rarely attract more than a tiny fraction of drivers; the majority of riders tend to come from other forms of public transit. The federal funding system, with its bias toward supporting big capital investments, has so encouraged rail projects as to lead many cities where rail makes no sense at all to apply for funds anyway, simply out of fear that they might be left out.

New rail systems from San Jose [California] to St. Louis [Missouri] have proven major disappointments. Strong early riderships have time and again faded as experience accumulates. Even Portland, [Oregon,] the poster child for public transit boosters, has seen its average commute times rise over the past decade and a half at one of the highest rates among American cities. Overall, the share of public transit use in the Portland region has not increased demonstrably over the past decade, despite heavy investment and draconian planning efforts to push residents out of private cars.

Nor have the downtowns of cities with expensive new rail systems seen the kind of resurgence transit boosters promise. Portland has not halted the flow of jobs and people out of its downtown. In fact, 90 percent of all new office space absorption in that city is now taking place outside the downtown core. . . .

If America is to accommodate the strong population and economic growth that lies in our near future, and still remain a highly mobile society, innovative thinking will be necessary. We must get beyond the notion of some mythical golden age. Forcing people to march back to an idealized early twentieth century pattern of dense, transit-dependent urbanity is not the solution.

Ultimately, our goal as a nation should be to create a more mobile society, one that allows ever greater choices for people to live how they wish, whether in a dense city, a decentralized suburb, the countryside, or some hybrid. Today, a false dichotomy is being foisted on the public which suggests their only options are either long highway commutes from anonymous exurbs, or being packed together in dense developments next to mass transit stations. Those are not choices we have to be limited to—if we will show the courage to say no to those who wish to drive us relentlessly back to a vanished past.

Periodical Bibliography

The following articles have been selected to supplement the diverse views presented in this chapter.

Mark Clayton — "Breaking Free from Energy Dependence," *USA Today*, October 22, 2004.

Aimee Cunningham — "Not-So-Clear Alternative," *Science News*, May 5, 2007.

Alan Drake — "Stop Ignoring Rail, America," *EVWorld*, July 10, 2007.

Economist — "Corn-Based Ethanol Not Cheap, Not Green," April 11, 2007.

Margaret Kriz — "Corn Power," *National Journal*, April 14, 2007.

Matthew S. Meisel — "Our Hang-up with Hydrogen," *Harvard Crimson*, September 20, 2006.

Spencer Reiss — "Why $5 Gas Is Good for America," *Wired*, December 2005.

Serge Schmemann — "I Love Paris on a Bus, a Bike, a Train and in Anything but a Car," *New York Times*, July 26, 2007.

John Semmens — "Missing the Bus: A Commentary," *Journal of Transportation Law*, vol. 4, 2006.

Samuel Staley — "Highways to Help," *New York Times*, August 5, 2007.

David Talbot — "Hell and Hydrogen," *Technology Review*, March 2007.

Lawrence Ulrich — "Green-Fuel Guide," *Popular Science*, May 2007.

USA Today — "Speed Public Transit," May 21, 2007.

Wall Street Journal — "Very, Very Big Corn," June 3, 2007.

CHAPTER 2

What Transportation Policies Best Protect National Security?

Chapter Preface

In 1961 following a series of hijackings to and from Cuba, the Federal Aviation Administration (FAA) permitted pilots to carry weapons, as long as the airline approved. In the decades that followed, relations with Cuba stabilized, the threat of hijacking diminished, and attitudes toward handguns chilled. By the late 1990s most airlines no longer permitted their pilots to carry weapons. The FAA officially removed its permission from aviation regulations in July 2001. The terrorist attacks of September 11 that same year renewed the debate over what strategies would best protect airline security. One of several controversial strategies to improve security aboard U.S. planes was to again allow airline pilots to arm themselves. Some commentators claim that arming pilots will improve the security of passengers on U.S. planes. Other analysts argue that armed pilots are a hazardous security strategy.

Those who support the arming of airline pilots see this strategy as a strong deterrent. The chief value of an armed pilot, these analysts assert, is to deter terrorists from getting on the plane in the first place. Senator Robert Smith maintains, "Armed pilots are a first line of deterrence to terrorism, because terrorists will know that armed pilots will be behind that reinforced cockpit door to defend the aircraft." Proponents contend that armed pilots are an added defense in a comprehensive range of security measures. A commentator from East Carolina University reasons, "Even if [terrorists] could get weapons past security, overcome air marshals, flight attendants and passengers, and penetrate the cockpit door, they would then find themselves staring down the barrel of a gun. That prospect would create a powerful incentive for terrorists to give up on the idea entirely."

Opponents claim that armed pilots increase the risks to passengers and crew. According to the Violence Policy Center

(VPS), "The [pilot's] gun, by definition, would potentially be available to every passenger, including those with a case of air rage or suffering from suicidal tendencies—as well as terrorists." In fact, VPS reasons, "Those contemplating terrorism will know that a gun is available and will act accordingly." To support their claim, VPS cites research in which 21 percent of highly trained police officers, whose only job is law enforcement, have been killed by their own weapon. A coalition of gun violence opponents argue that arming pilots will unnecessarily increase flight crew stress. "While flight crews should certainly be given the tools necessary to keep them and their planes safe from danger, including terrorists, we must also consider the serious ramifications of compounding existing stresses with the additional burden of acting as law-enforcement officers on flights."

Whether armed pilots are an effective or dangerous airline security strategy remains the subject of rigorous debate. The authors in the following chapter explore other controversies in the debate over which transportation security policies are best.

| "Only by privatizing . . . security can we . . . let those who have an actual stake in safety be charged with protecting passengers."

Privatizing Airport Security Will Better Protect Passengers

Anthony Gregory

The private sector is in the best position to protect the security of airline passengers, argues Anthony Gregory in the following viewpoint. Unlike the government, he asserts, the private sector has more incentive to protect airline passengers. The private sector must compete for consumer dollars to avoid bankruptcy, Gregory claims, and unlike the government, can be held liable for its actions. Moreover, he maintains, private businesses lose money when their customers are mistreated, as they often are by government airport security employees. Gregory is a research analyst at the Independent Institute, a libertarian think tank.

As you read, consider the following questions:

1. According to Gregory, what are the only endeavors un-encumbered by politicization?

Anthony Gregory, "Time to Depoliticize Airline Security," *Independent Institute*, August 30, 2006. Copyright © 2006. Reproduced by permission of The *Independent Institute*, 100 Swan Way, Oakland, CA 94021-1428 USA. www.independent.org.

2. What examples does the author cite to support his claim that government airline security is ineffective?

3. In the author's view, why does the government have no institutional incentive to protect passengers?

Upon the [2006] discovery of an alleged plot to terrorize airplanes flying from Britain to the United States, the Transportation Security Administration (TSA) rapidly prohibited commercial airline passengers from bringing fluids— bottled water, soft drinks, shampoo, and other liquid toiletries—onto planes.

Some critics of the new TSA policy have questioned the immediacy with which the new, sweeping restrictions were issued. The suspects who were supposedly going to sneak liquid explosives onto a plane did not have tickets yet, and some did not even have passports, which in Britain require months of waiting. According to NBC News, "one senior British official suggested an attack was not imminent."

The Politicization of Security

President [George W.] Bush's critics complain that the new TSA restrictions were based more on politics than real security concerns, but they should not be surprised. The only endeavors unencumbered by politicization are those that are free from political decision-making—those separated from the state. After [the terrorist attacks of] 9/11, airline security was nationalized. Democrats were the first to insist on the change; Republicans initially resisted, but ultimately backed it.

Government airline security has been burdensome, bizarre and ineffective. In 2003, college student Nathaniel Heatwole smuggled box cutters onto two airplanes. Several media exposés have demonstrated the inconsistency of security at checkpoints, through which thousands of people sneak prohibited items every year. Countless flights have been delayed and passengers dramatically inconvenienced by ridiculous

shutdowns of airport gates, all because some agent found a pair of scissors in a trashcan or thought someone looked suspicious.

Rarely does anyone ask what makes airplanes so much more vulnerable to bombings than office buildings, restaurants, theaters, and other crowded places. Why all the focus on airport security lines, rather than the many other sectors of the busy society? If the unique danger is supposedly that planes can be hijacked and used as missiles as they were on 9/11, why not allow airlines to protect themselves by arming their pilots or even allowing armed passengers? The airlines have every incentive to protect their customers, employees and investments, and can determine the best way to do so.

Airlines could have different standards, and customers could choose which ones to patronize—those that allow firearms or those that disarm their passengers and crew; those that scrutinize all patrons equally or those that are more cautious with passengers of a statistically riskier demographic.

Car insurance companies make distinctions on the basis of demographics. Why can't airlines?

Public vs. Private Incentives

We could expect some differences in the way the private and public sectors would handle a possible threat. People in the private sector, whether individual passengers or airline companies, are held liable for their actions. Businesses lose money when they don't protect their assets, and they go under if they abuse their customers the way TSA frequently mistreats travelers. Private individuals tend to be measured and effective even in responding to such serious threats as Richard Reid, the shoe-bomber, who in December 2001 got past government security only to be neutralized by flight attendants and passengers aboard the plane.

The government, in contrast, has no liability when something goes wrong. And so after two U.S. Air Marshals gunned down Rigoberto Alpizar as he ran off his scheduled flight at Miami International Airport on December 7, 2005, there was no effort to change security policy—only an attempt by officials all the way up to President Bush to whitewash what had happened. After government claims that Alpizar had shouted out he had a bomb were contradicted by every single passenger on board and after it was shown the unarmed man had no terrorist connections whatsoever, government officials faced no consequences for the deadly overreaction and cover-up that followed.

Indeed, the government, unlike private enterprise, has no institutional incentive to protect passengers. It does not fear bankruptcy, lawsuits, prosecution or even competition. Rather, the government uses airline security as just another way to expand its size and power. Every terrorist attack, potential or successful, translates into bigger bureaucratic budgets. Failure is rewarded with more money. The occasional atrocity, such as the killing of Alpizar, is seen as the price we pay to be safe.

It should be no wonder, then, that the norm at the airports is intimidation, onerous hassle, fear of officials, as though one were in a police state, and, at best, a false sense of security against terrorists. Only by privatizing and deregulating security can we depoliticize it and let those who have an actual stake in safety be charged with protecting passengers.

"*It hardly matters who wears the [airport security] uniform if employees don't get the tools they need.*"

Privatization Will Not Resolve Airport Security Challenges

Paul C. Light

Privatizing airport security will not resolve the challenges faced by the Transportation Security Administration (TSA), claims Paul C. Light in the following viewpoint. The federal government created TSA to take over U.S. airport security following the terrorist attacks of September 11, 2001, but congressional funding cuts and employee caps in the years following the terrorist attacks have made it difficult for the TSA to meet new security challenges, Light argues. Neither private nor government airport security will improve without adequate training and technology, he maintains. Light is a fellow at the Brookings Institution, a liberal think tank in Washington, DC.

As you read, consider the following questions:

1. In Light's opinion, in what remarkable ways did the TSA respond to its urgent mission?

Paul C. Light, "Still Searching for Airport Security: Wasn't TSA Going to Be the Solution?" www.brookings.edu, June 12, 2007. Reproduced by permission of the author.

2. How did cuts and caps impact the TSA, according to the author?

3. Why, in the author's view, are private firms not anxious to enter the competition?

It was created to shield the nation's airports and transportation systems from attack after Sept. 11, 2001. But lately, the Transportation Security Administration (TSA) itself has come under more scrutiny than a cigarette lighter at a passenger screening station.

The ... agency has been ridiculed for everything from pat-downs of women and U.S. senators, to a "no-fly" passenger list that has produced story after story of mistaken identity, to a ... $16 million purchase of new uniforms with sturdier epaulets. More importantly, it still fails too often at detecting guns, knives and improvised explosive devices, and it's years behind in developing "smart" technologies that could help screeners do their work. . . .

The Story of the TSA

The story of TSA can serve as a classic Washington morality tale. The agency is one of the federal government's greatest bureaucratic achievements of the past 50 years. But it's also an embodiment of the torpor that can overcome bureaucracies, public or private. As memories of 9/11 have faded, TSA has begun to look like any other federal agency. It has lived an entire bureaucratic life in quick time, moving from urgency toward complacency in just three short years [from 2002 to 2005]. The question now is whether it can make up in time to prevent its own demise.

Given an urgent mission and almost no time to achieve it, TSA grew from just 13 federal employees in January 2002 to nearly 65,000 by the following November. That's not only remarkable, it's unprecedented. It met every deadline in a deadline-heavy statute, built screening stations on every concourse at every commercial airport and fired the private screeners who had been on duty the day terrorists turned four airplanes into massive bombs. Just 18 months after its launch, TSA moved into the new Department of Homeland Security as one of its anchor agencies.

But TSA's extraordinary achievements didn't insulate it from anti-big-government attacks from House Republicans who opposed the agency from the start. Nor did they prevent standard bureaucratic blunders, such as lavish spending on executive office furniture.

It's easy to blame those House Republicans—who never met a TSA budget they couldn't cut and eventually capped the number of screeners at 45,000 in 2003—for the tailspin. The cuts and caps not only distracted the agency from more important problems, such as port security, but they also delayed the development of new technologies that might have helped employees wade through X-rays of cluttered carry-on baggage and eliminate the much-reviled pat-downs. TSA also had little choice but to fill the gaps with temporary employees, summer replacements and part-timers, and to carve into its research and development budget to meet the inevitable payroll short-falls. It also put those less-than-smiley private contractors at the front of the waiting lines to check tickets and IDs, and even imposed a temporary hiring freeze during the heavy 2003 season.

The Struggles Within

But not all of the turbulence came from outside the agency. Driven by the demand for consistency where none had existed before, as well as by his own history in federal law enforcement, TSA's first administrator, John Magaw, issued one irritating rule after another, prohibiting passengers from carrying nail clippers through checkpoints one day, and cups of coffee the next.

With just 1,200 screeners in place by June 1, 2002, and TSA's airport directors in near revolt against his one-size-fits-all-airports approach, Magaw was replaced late that summer by former Coast Guard commandant James Loy, a no-nonsense administrator who had once admonished [former president] Bill Clinton that the logical extension of doing more with less was doing everything with nothing. Within three months of Loy's arrival, the coffee rule was gone, airline employees stopped asking that ridiculous question about never leaving your suitcase alone, and the agency was hiring 8,000 to 10,000 screeners a month.

Yet Loy's honeymoon was not to last. Already operating under the employment cap, and facing a second year of budget cuts from the White House, TSA saw employee turnover and worker injuries begin to rise. Performance stagnated—and rumors of dismantling began flying.

Loy also made the unenviable decision to prohibit labor organizing. Although Congress would have made the decision for him if he hadn't, the move created endless complaints on the frontlines, especially in a workplace where pilots, flight attendants, mechanics and baggage handlers are all unionized. Having interviewed more then my share of passenger screeners over the years, I know firsthand about the anger. Every time I ask a screener about the labor issue on my travels, I get pulled aside for an extra-thorough pat-down. I don't know whether they think I'm pro-management or just asking too many questions, but the result is almost always 10 more minutes with the security screener.

The Future of Transportation Security

TSA faces several possible futures. If House GOP [Republican Party] members get their way, for example, the agency will become what they always wanted—a small regulatory agency with limited oversight responsibility over private contractors. So far, there's no sign of a mad rush toward privatizing the

TSA Successes

TSA's highly trained security officers have successfully mini-mized passenger wait times at security checkpoints even with air travel back to pre-9/11 levels.

Over 40 million prohibited items have been intercepted at screening checkpoints since TSA assumed responsibility for security at the nation's 450 airports in February of 2002. . . .

TSA has substantially bolstered intelligence gathering and is aggressively pursuing new and/or improved technol-ogy. Approximately $1 billion has been committed to up-grading explosives detection systems at airports over a three-year period.

In January 2004, TSA doubled the Artesia, N.M.–based training program for arming pilots, both passenger and cargo, to defend the cockpit as Federal Flight Deck Officers. There are currently several thousand trained officers.

Transportation Security Administration, 2007.

airport security job again. Although Congress allowed airports to opt out of the federal system in favor of private contractors beginning November [2004], only the airport in tiny Elko, Nev., has asked TSA to approve the changeover.

Nor are private firms particularly anxious to enter the competition. It's one thing to try making money when wages start at $5.15 an hour and a job at Cinnabon is a promotion, as former senator Max Cleland once so memorably suggested. It's quite another to try making money when wages start at $11.30 an hour plus training and benefits. Private firms also rightly wonder whether current federal liability caps would actually hold in the event of another security breakdown, and whether TSA would be a particularly encouraging partner, having been stripped of yet another responsibility.

But it hardly matters who wears the uniform if employees don't get the tools they need. Given the same pay, training and technology, private screeners in San Francisco, Kansas City and the three other airports Congress allowed TSA to leave in private hands have been only slightly more effective at detecting threats than federal screeners. And absent significant investment in new technologies, they won't reach perfection, either.

A New Business Model

What TSA desperately needs is a new business model that will reassure its critics and increase screener performance. It needs to be more alert to new threats, such as the strap-on explosives used by Chechen rebels to bring down two Russian airplanes [in 2004]; more agile in meeting the inevitable surge of passengers that comes with the changing travel season and the movement of high-volume carriers such as Southwest into underused hubs; and more innovative in funding screening technologies that can be used in a variety of public and private settings beyond airports. Meanwhile, it needs to concentrate fire on the nation's most vulnerable airport terminals. Reagan National's Terminal C, for example, has plenty of room for leisurely passenger screening, but Terminal A has a bottleneck that puts enormous pressure on screeners to get passengers through as fast as possible. Guess which one a terrorist would pick.

Building this kind of robust, risk-focused TSA would require more than new uniforms, obviously. It requires a mindset that harks back to the glory days of the National Aeronautics and Space Administration (NASA), which was established in 1958 during a similar moment of great urgency. Also operating under personnel and budget caps, NASA created new incentives for private investment in a host of new technologies that helped build a base for decades of innovation.

TSA's challenge is to avoid the fate of NASA, which has been marked by tragedy and is mired in uncertainty about its mission. If its screeners stay federal, TSA could easily end up like the U.S. Postal Service, with its predictable, if sometimes underwhelming, performance. If the screeners go private, it could end up as just another starving regulatory agency like the Occupational Safety and Health Administration.

The public will be poorly served under either scenario. TSA needs to become a more agile, adaptable version of its former self, which will require a round of internal reorganization that will make its first year seem like a cakewalk. But if the agency can pull it off, it could yet become one of the government's greatest bureaucratic achievements of the *next* 50 years.

> *"Human trafficking, drugs and smuggling all flourish thanks to the lax standards of shipping ports and the scant resources made available to police them."*

The United States Should Maintain Control of Ports

The Nation

Critical infrastructure such as U.S. ports should remain in the hands of American-controlled companies, as opposed to the Dubai Ports World, according to the following viewpoint. Since other critical American assets such as domestic airlines require that top management must be U.S. citizens, the same should be true of U.S. ports. The Nation *is a liberal news and opinion weekly.*

As you read, consider the following questions:

1. Since 9/11, how much money has been spent on port security compared to airports, according to the *Nation*?

2. According to the authors, why should Americans revolt against the Dubai Ports World contract?

3. Why is the Dubai Ports World considered a scandal, in the opinion of the authors?

Rise by fear, fall by fear. Having deliberately nurtured a national security panic for the past four-plus years, President George W. Bush richly deserves to be trampled in its latest running: the uproar over his Administration's decision to hand management of six US ports to a state-owned Dubai firm. Bush is cornered by his own bulls—Bill Frist and Dennis Hastert warning darkly of national security threats implied by Arab ownership of American ports, other Republicans accusing him of coddling Dubai's state-socialist enterprise. Democrats, seeing a weakened President, pile gleefully on, but they, too, seem unconcerned about the corrosive implications of national security scares and economic xenophobia.

Although the Coast Guard reportedly warned the President that gaps in intelligence make the risks in the deal involving Dubai Ports [DP] World hard to evaluate, the question of mangement-company ownership has little to do with genuine security issues, since the ports are policed by the Guard, Customs and Homeland Security.

Poor Port Management

The more important public safety problem, as Senator Carl Levin points out with welcome sanity, is that the Administration has long treated the nation's ports as the poor stepchild of transportation security. Of 11 million containers shipped through US ports annually, 95 percent are never inspected or opened; and since the attacks of 9/11 just $630 million has been spent on port security, compared with $18 billion for airports. Human trafficking, drugs and smuggling all flourish thanks to the lax standards of shipping ports and the scant resources made available to police them.

And foreign management of ports is nothing new. The work crews who load and unload vessels in American harbors

U.S. Seaport Security	
Major shipping ports in the U.S.	361
Cargo containers that arrive daily in U.S. ports	21,000
U.S. imports that arrive via cargo ship	95%
Foreign cargo ships that dock in the U.S. every year	8,000
Warterborne cargo regularly inspected upon entry in the U.S	6%
According to one security expert, ships in possession of the Al Qaeda terrorist group	30

TAKEN FROM: "U.S. Seaport Security," *Issues and Controversies*, February 18, 2005.

already draw their paychecks from companies based in Singapore, Denmark, the United Kingdom, Japan and Taiwan. Is DP World more likely to support terrorism than British-owned P&O? No, and thus an unmistakable whiff of anti-Arab bigotry wafts from the argument.

So what's really at stake? It's another case of Democrats and Republicans alike happily promoting corporate globalism with little regard for the public interest until the implications become too embarrassing: in this case, the control of the nation's ports being traded by transnational corporations. If Americans should revolt against the DP World contract it's not because investors come from unpopular places like China or Dubai but for the same reasons that Bolivians revolted against Bechtel Corporation's takeover of water utilities: because American harbors should not be just another commodity to be traded like cotton futures. Rather, they are the people's birthright, as crucial to the transportation infrastructure and economy as highways and airports. It's there that Congressional Democrats should be taking their stand. Yet which Democrat has the nerve to call for a public takeover of the ports?

Dubai Deal Is a National Security Threat

It's hard not to cheer as the DP World fight blows a big hole in what's left of the Bush Administration agenda, but we must realize that by framing the Dubai deal as a national security threat, Democrats are paradoxically reinforcing Bush's master narrative of a permanent and all-encompassing "war on terror." They are also dangerously enhancing the equation of Islam with terrorism that Bush so deftly exploited to launch the Iraq War.

Democrats should see the panic over the DP World deal as an opportunity for a truly nervy rudder-turn—challenging the toxic premises of Bush's national security policy and confronting the obsession with secrecy that led to the consummation of the deal out of sight of Congress. The Dubai Ports World scandal is a scandal—but mainly because it is the latest chapter in this Administration's ongoing, sweeping betrayal of the public interest. Playing to fear is a mug's game that only Bush can win.

"*Management companies that run ports do not control security. The U.S. Coast Guard controls the physical security of our ports.*"

Outsourcing Port Management Will Not Threaten National Security

The Washington Post

Having a foreign company manage U.S. ports will not threaten national security, claim the editors of the Washington Post. *In fact, they argue, the U.S. Coast Guard and the U.S. Customs Service control port security, not port management companies. Moreover, the authors assert, the United States should promote the economic integration of Arab countries to encourage democracy in the Middle East. Indeed, the authors maintain, Dubai Ports World, the company approved to take over management of U.S. ports, is based in the United Arab Emirates, a U.S. ally.*

As you read, consider the following questions:

1. According to the *Washington Post*, who is Britain as likely to harbor as Dubai?

2. In what ways has the United Arab Emirates cooperated with the United States, in the opinion of the authors?

3. In the authors' view, what is one of the basic goals of contemporary U.S. foreign policy?

You know there's something suspicious going on when multiple members of Congress—House, Senate, Democrat, Republican, future presidential candidates of all stripes—spontaneously unite around an issue that none of them had known existed a week earlier. That appears to be what happened [in February 2006] after politicians awoke to the fairly stale news that the London-based P&O navigation company, which has long managed the ports of New York, New Jersey, Baltimore, New Orleans, Miami and Philadelphia, had been taken over by Dubai Ports World, a company based in the United Arab Emirates. Sen. Lindsey O. Graham (R-S.C.) called the deal "tone-deaf politically at this point in our history." Senate Majority Leader Bill Frist (R-Tenn.) called for the White House to put a hold on the purchase. Minority Leader Harry M. Reid (D-Nev.) seconded him, implying that Arab owners posed a major security threat—as did everyone from Sen. Hillary Rodham Clinton (D-N.Y.) to Sen. Charles E. Schumer (D-N.Y.) to Rep. Peter T. King (R-N.Y.) to Maryland Gov. Robert L. Ehrlich Jr. (R).

Misunderstanding Port Management

At stake—in theory—is the question of whether we should "outsource major port security to a foreign-based company," in the words of Mr. Graham. But those words, like those of almost all of the others, sound, well, tone-deaf to us. For one, the deal cannot "outsource major port security," because management companies that run ports do not control security. The U.S. Coast Guard controls the physical security of our ports. The U.S. Customs Service controls container security. That doesn't change, no matter who runs the business operations. Nor is it clear why Mr. Graham or anybody else should

Security Standards Will Not Change

The U.S. Coast Guard is responsible for overseeing the implementation of ISPS [International Shipping and Port Security code]. Every U.S. port has a Coast Guard officer who is the Captain of the Port and is responsible for coordinating all port security. The Customs and Border Protection agency and the Coast Guard, not the owner of the port, conduct security screening on individuals and cargo that enter the port.

James Jay Carafano and Alane Kochems,
The Heritage Foundation, February 22, 2006.

be worried about "foreign-based" companies managing U.S. ports, since P&O is a British company. And Britain, as events of [2005] have illustrated, is no less likely to harbor radical Islamic terrorists than Dubai.

None of the U.S. politicians huffing and puffing seem to be aware that this deal was long in the making, that it had been reported on extensively in the financial press, and that it went through normal security clearance procedures, including approval from a foreign investment committee that contains officials from the departments of Treasury, Commerce, State and Homeland Security, among other agencies. Even more disturbing is the apparent difficulty of members of Congress in distinguishing among Arab countries. We'd like to remind them, as they've apparently forgotten, that the United Arab Emirates is a U.S. ally that has cooperated extensively with U.S. security operations in the war on terrorism, that supplied troops to the U.S.-led coalition during the 1991 Persian Gulf War, and that sends humanitarian aid to Iraq. U.S. troops move freely in and out of Dubai on their way to Iraq now.

Finally, we're wondering if perhaps American politicians are having trouble understanding some of the most basic goals of contemporary U.S. foreign policy. A goal of "democracy promotion" in the Middle East, after all, is to encourage Arab countries to become economically and politically integrated with the rest of the world. What better way to do so than by encouraging Arab companies to invest in the United States? Clearly, Congress doesn't understand that basic principle, since its members prefer instead to spread prejudice and misinformation.

| "*[The NAFTA Superhighway] will not be secured, and the result . . . would be the . . . obliteration of the current national borders.*"

The NAFTA Superhighway Threatens U.S. Sovereignty and Security

Kelly Taylor

According to Kelly Taylor in the following viewpoint, policy makers who hope to merge Canada, the United States, and Mexico into a North American Union are planning a chain of transportation corridors that will stretch from Mexico to Canada. This North American Free Trade Agreement (NAFTA) Superhighway will erase U.S. borders, she claims, threatening U.S. sovereignty and security. Not only will U.S. taxpayers pay for this superhighway, she asserts, they will also sacrifice their land, farms, and jobs. Taylor is a writer, filmmaker, and producer of a political TV talk show.

As you read, consider the following questions:

1. What does Taylor cite as evidence that the superhighway is a plan to do away with U.S. borders?

Kelly Taylor, "Coming Through! The NAFTA Super Highway," www.jbs.org, August 20, 2007. Reproduced by permission.

2. Why has the proposed North American Union gone virtually unnoticed, in the author's opinion?

3. What, in the author's view, will be the impact of wedding Mexico's cheap labor force with the new infrastructure?

All across America, mammoth construction projects are preparing to launch. The NAFTA Super Highway is on a fast track and it's headed your way. If you don't help derail it, you may soon be run over by it—both figuratively and literally.

The NAFTA Super Highway is a venture unlike any previous highway construction project. It is actually a daisy chain of dozens of corridors and coordinated projects that are expected to stretch out for several decades, cost *hundreds of billions* of dollars, and end up radically reconfiguring not only the physical landscape of these United States, but our political and economic landscapes as well.

In Texas, the NAFTA Super Highway is being sold as the Trans Texas Corridor [TTC]. In simplest terms, the TTC is a superhighway system including tollways for passenger vehicles and trucks; lanes for commercial and freight trucks; tracks for commuter rail and high-speed freight rail; depots for all rail lines; pipelines for oil, water, and natural gas; and electrical towers and cabling for communication and telephone lines. One of the proposed corridor routes, TTC-35, is parallel to the present Interstate Highway 35 (I-35), slightly to the east, running north from Mexico to Canada. Its present scope is 4,000 miles long, 1,200 feet wide, with an estimated cost of $183 *billion* of taxpayer funds. It runs through Kansas City.

Integration vs. Independence

How would all of this affect you, your family, and your community? Let us count the ways. One of the most striking features of the proposed Super Highway is the plan to do away with our borders, as evidenced by the joint U.S.-Mexico Customs facility already under construction in Kansas City, Missouri. A U.S. Customs checkpoint in Kansas City? But that's a thousand miles inside America's heartland; isn't the purpose of U.S. Customs to check people and cargo at our borders?

Ah, but the mere asking of that question shows that you're still operating under the *old* paradigm that sees the United States as an independent, sovereign nation. However, that paradigm began to change following passage of the North American Free Trade Agreement (NAFTA) in 1994. NAFTA, which was sold to the American public as a simple trade agreement, was actually far more than that, setting in motion a process for the gradual social, economic, and political "integration," or merger, of the three NAFTA countries—Canada, the United States, and Mexico—into a North American Union.

In 2005, this merger process became more explicit and aggressive when President [George W.] Bush, Mexico's President Vicente Fox, and Canada's Prime Minister [Paul] Martin launched what they call the Security and Prosperity Partnership of North America (SPP). Any serious study of the SPP will clearly reveal that its ultimate aim is the dissolution of the United States into a North American Union patterned after the increasingly dictatorial regional government now running the European Union. Henceforth, under this plan, the borders between our nations will be incrementally erased in favor of a joint "perimeter" around all three countries.

One part of this plan calls for streamlining the flow of traffic from Mexico, including a massive increase in containers from China and the Far East offloading at Mexican seaports and then being transported by truck and rail into the United States via the new NAFTA Super Highway. These new cargo streams would cross the border in supposedly secure FAST lanes, checked only electronically until the first Customs stop in Kansas City!

What about all the repeated promises by the White House and Congress to make border security America's "top priority"? Moving Customs inspections hundreds of miles inland obviously contradicts those promises and incalculably increases the opportunities for smugglers (of drugs, illegal aliens, terrorists, weapons of mass destruction, and other contraband) to enter the country. Our borders are already incredibly porous and undermanned; securing the entire route from the Mexico-Texas border to Kansas City would require *thousands* more Border Patrol and Customs officers. Would these agents be provided? Could this route be made any more secure than our southern border? Does it make sense to effectively extend the border via this route when we are now doing such a poor job securing our existing border?

Under the Radar

Moreover, we can expect that similar inland joint Customs facilities, like the one in Kansas City, will be included in the other Mexico-to-Canada superhighway corridors. Of course, these corridors will not be secured, and the result—as intended—would be the *de facto* merger of immigration and Customs enforcement and the obliteration of the current national borders within the planned North American Union. That is precisely what one of the main architects of the SPP plan, Professor Robert Pastor of American University and the Council on Foreign Relations, has repeatedly advocated in his writings, speeches, and congressional testimony.

How is it possible that something this radical has gone so far virtually unnoticed when illegal immigration and border security are among the hottest political topics of the day? The politicians and the private contractors who have been pushing this merger scheme intended it that way, knowing full well that adoption and successful implementation of the plan would depend on keeping it under the public radar.

Thanks largely to the investigative work of Joyce Mucci, who heads the Kansas City–based Mid-America Immigration Reform Coalition, and author/economist Jerome Corsi, the NAFTA Super Highway has begun to be a very hot topic. Using Missouri's Sunshine Law, Mrs. Mucci's group has pried loose a number of documents that are causing the public and private champions of the NAFTA Super Highway to squirm and stonewall. "They were going along great guns with this whole plan, with all of their high-powered politicians, law firms, PR [public relations] firms, and corporate contractors—and virtually no opposition, until now," Mrs. Mucci told *The New American*. "We're just volunteers, so we don't have the money and influence they have, but we are digging out the truth." And she is hopeful that if enough taxpayers, voters, and property owners learn about all the horrendous ramifications of the Super Highway plan, they will shut it down before it can do the damage envisioned.

Super Highway Robbery

Aside from erasing our borders—which is no small matter in and of itself—the NAFTA Super Highway would profoundly impact Americans in many other ways. The ones who will be most immediately affected are those whose homes, farms, ranches, businesses, and communities lay in the paths of any of the planned routes. Millions of acres are scheduled to be paved over and that means using eminent domain to condemn lots of private property for the Super Highway corridors and rights-of-way.

But *every* American, ultimately, would be dramatically impacted by this onrushing scheme. How? First of all, in the pocketbook—with increased taxes and tolls. With an aggregate price tag of hundreds of billions of dollars—for projects in the U.S. and Mexico—enormous increases in federal, state, and local taxes are a certainty. To assist in financing the mammoth Super Highway, plans call for converting many current roads, which taxpayers have already paid for, to tollways for all motor vehicles.

If the NAFTA Super Highway goes through as planned, millions of Americans can expect to pay with their jobs as well. Just as the NAFTA trade policies have driven millions of jobs out of the United States, the NAFTA Super Highway will accelerate the job exodus. Although the Super Highway corridors are being sold locally as projects to ease congestion and facilitate U.S. economic competitiveness, their main purpose, very clearly, is to create an arterial network for speeding the delivery of manufactured products *into* the United States through Canada and Mexico.

Thus, U.S. taxpayers would have to pay for reduced transportation costs for foreign producers. In addition, the "continental" plan calls for U.S. taxpayers to pay hundreds of billions of dollars to extend this "infrastructure development" (highways, railways, bridges, power plants, telecommunications, seaports) through Mexico and Central America.

How will it do that? Under the Coordinated Border Infrastructure Program of the Safe, Accountable, Flexible, Efficient Transportation Equity Act of 2005—A Legacy for Users (SAFETEA-LU) (whew!), U.S. funds apportioned to a border state may be used to construct a highway project in Canada or Mexico, if that project directly facilitates cross-border vehicle and cargo movement! Just think—your tax dollars may now be sent to Canada or Mexico to aid the entry of illegal aliens into the United States, like it or not.

Additionally, SAFETEA-LU allows U.S. states to use tolling on a pilot basis to finance Interstate construction and reconstruction, and to establish tolls for *existing* Interstate highways to fund the new Super Highway corridors. Austin, Texas, is already experiencing fierce struggles over converting its *already-paid-for* Interstate and state highways to toll roads, but few Texans understand that this new tolling is to be the mecha-

The Abolition of Sovereignty

The ultimate goal [of the NAFTA Superhighway] is not simply a superhighway, but an integrated North American Union—complete with a currency, a cross-national bureaucracy, and virtually borderless travel within the Union. Like the European Union, a North American Union would represent another step toward the abolition of national sovereignty altogether.

Ron Paul, Lew Rockwell.com, October 31, 2006.

nism for funding the leviathan Trans Texas Corridor. Since Austin has been identified as the pilot city *in the nation* for testing the new toll policies, you can assume that what passes here is coming your way.

This planned wedding of Mexico's cheap labor force with brand new infrastructure would make Mexico an irresistible magnet for all manufacturers now remaining in the United States. Even those companies who wanted to keep their operations here would likely be forced by cheaper competitors to join the exodus. The United States, until very recently the manufacturing capital of the world, will continue its downward spiral into increasingly dangerous dependence on foreign manufacturers for almost everything, even as burgeoning inflation makes everything more expensive, devastating much of our middle class. . . .

Scores of Corridors

An additional Super Highway route known as the Interstate 69 corridor (TTC-69) would enter Texas from Mexico as three spur lines at Laredo, McAllen, and Brownsville, which then will join together to head north through Houston, to Memphis, Tennessee, to Port Huron, Michigan, to Toronto, Canada.

Wait, there's more. To the west of the proposed TTC lies the proposed route of the Ports-to-Plains Corridor, running north from Laredo through West Texas, the Oklahoma Panhandle, to Denver and ultimately Canada. What? Another one? Yes, and plans are very advanced. Its website identifies this corridor as a NAFTA corridor alternative to TTC-35, the one paralleling I-35.

What does the Texas Department of Transportation (TxDOT) have to say about this? Once again, stonewalling rules. In telephone interviews with congenial TxDOT employees, the expected mantra repeated to this writer is how necessary the corridor is to accommodate projected population and trade growth, and how beneficial it would be to the economies of Texas, the U.S., and Mexico. TxDOT's Public Information officer denied that the TTC was part of any bigger scheme of nationwide corridor building, and claimed that notion was simply misinformation. Yet in a June 30, 2001 article in the *Austin American Statesman*, the same spokesperson claimed the aforementioned Ports-to-Plains Corridor would be linked to existing Interstate highways in Denver as part of a NAFTA super corridor.

And that's not all. There's also CANAMEX, another super corridor like the TTC, which spans the West from Mexico to Canada going through Arizona, Nevada, Utah, Idaho, and Montana. And we learn from the CANAMEX Corridor Coalition website that the number of *congressionally* designated high priority corridors in the United States has been expanded from 43 to 80! Yes, 80 corridor routes have been designated across the United States in an effort to speed the construction of infrastructure necessary for what the SPP calls "the streamlined movement of legitimate travelers and cargo across our shared borders."

Research on any High Priority Corridor will lead the reader into a hairball of studies, alliances, pricing programs, transportation acts, administration agencies, reports, committees, partnerships, and on and on, all designed, we believe, to obscure the real agenda. The idea for these 80 super corridors was not conceived to promote trade and better the economic development of all participating communities. When viewed in the aggregate, they can only be seen as a means to so thoroughly restructure and integrate the three countries so as to permanently blur the distinctions, and to make their merger into a regional government seamless and even appealing.

The NAFTA Super Highway is such an integral part of the continental merger plan that the entire scheme could be at least temporarily road-blocked if it does not proceed. If it does proceed, American government will no longer provide its time-tested protections against tyranny and socialism, as huge chunks of American law will be rendered void, and replaced by an incomprehensible mess of "trade" law. All rowers are needed at the oars, and immediately. If you've asked yourself why you did not know about a project of this magnitude, or where Congress got the authority to designate High Priority Corridors in the first place, your first job is to contact your representative and howl. Wake the town and tell the people, or the town will be paved over.

> *"There is absolutely no US government plan for a NAFTA Superhighway of any sort."*

The NAFTA Superhighway Is an Unsubstantiated Rumor

Philip Dine

The rumor that policy makers hoping to create a North American Union are planning a NAFTA Superhighway that will connect Canada, the United States, and Mexico is unfounded, asserts Philip Dine in the following viewpoint. The rumor, made widely available on the Internet, is being fueled by those who fear globalization and immigration, he claims. The goal of those who hope to improve America's major trade corridors in the Midwest is to reduce the cost of trade and improve border security, not undermine American sovereignty, Dine asserts. Dine writes for the St. Louis Post-Dispatch.

As you read, consider the following questions:

1. According to Dine, what do those who believe that there is a conspiracy to merge Canada, the United States, and Mexico cite as proof?

2. In the author's opinion, what efforts do those who believe in a NAFTA Superhighway refer to in an attempt to prove that the government is not telling the truth?

3. As cited by DIne, what does Michael Barkun claim is a major theme of many conspiracy theories?

Forget conspiracy theories about JFK's [John F. Kennedy] assassination, black helicopters, Sept. 11, 2001. This is the big one.

We're talking about the secret plan to build a superhighway, a giant 10- to 12-lane production, from the Yucatan to the Yukon. This "SuperCorridor" would allow the really big part of the plan to take place: the merging of the governments of Canada, the United States and Mexico. Say goodbye to the dollar, and maybe even the English language.

The rumor is sweeping the Internet, radio and magazines, spread by bloggers, broadcasters and writers who cite the "proof" in the writings of a respected American University professor, in a task force put together by the Council on Foreign Relations and in the workings of the Commerce Department.

As do many modern rumors, fears of a North American Union [NAU] began with a few grains of truth and leapt to an unsubstantiated conclusion.

Back and Forth

"There is absolutely no US government plan for a NAFTA Superhighway of any sort," said David Bohigian, an assistant secretary of commerce. Sen. Kit Bond, R-Mo., a powerful member of committees that would authorize and pay for a North American Free Trade Agreement Superhighway if one were being planned, dismissed the notion as "unfounded theories" with "no credence."

And yet: A pending congressional resolution condemns it. Rep. Ron Paul, R-Texas, speaks darkly of "secret funding" for it. Commentators fulminate against the four-football-fields-wide behemoth as a threat to private property, national security and "a major lifeline of the plan to merge the United States into a North American Community," as conservative activist Phyllis Schlafly wrote.

Conservative commentator Pat Buchanan writes that under the North American Union plan, "the illegal-alien invasion would be solved by eliminating America's borders and legalizing the invasion."

Congressional Action

Responding to denials, Rep Virgil Goode, R-Va, the chief sponsor of the House of Representatives resolution opposing the NAFTA Superhighway, scoffed: "I've heard that line before. They're just calling it something else. . . . It's a decrease in our security and an erasing of our borders."

Goode is hardly alone: His resolution has attracted 21 co-sponsors, from both parties.

"Nobody is proposing a North American Union," countered Robert Pastor, the American University professor to whom conspiracy theorists point as "the father of the NAU." They cite his 2001 book, *Towards a North American Community: Lessons from the Old World for the New* as the basic text for the plan. They also note his co-chairmanship of a Council on Foreign Relations task force that produced a 2005 report on cooperation among the three countries.

This is no backwoods rumor, no small-time concern. Google "North American Union" on the Internet and you'll find 113 million references (as of [May 2007]).

Stoking Fears

On one . . . day alone, Pastor said, he received 100 e-mails on the topic. "They get turned on by [CNN's] Lou Dobbs and [Fox's] Bill O'Reilly, who are fearful that Mexicans and Canadians are about to take over our country," Pastor said, adding that such claims are a product of "the xenophobic or frightened right wing of America that is afraid of immigration and globalization."

Not that he doesn't think cooperation—short of a merger—is a good idea. He has testified before Congress on improving coordination within North America.

"The three governments are trying to grope toward a better way to relate to one another, but they are trying to do it under the radar screen, because they know any initiative would be both controversial and difficult to get approval of," Pastor said. "But precisely because they're doing it so quietly, the conservative crowd is concerned that they're really doing something important. But they're not. The real problem is that the three governments are asleep on the issue."

Tom Fitton is president of Judicial Watch, a conservative group that promotes accountability in government. He said his group was "investigating" the rumors and that, while it hadn't uncovered proof positive, the [George W.] Bush administration was fueling suspicion by the way it was handling the issue.

"You've got all these ministries in the three countries working trilaterally on transportation, energy, food safety, health, pandemics and border security," Fitton said. "The concern from some on the right is that the process is not as transparent as it ought to be, and that it is a threat to sovereignty in the sense that they're talking about integration instead of just cooperation."

The supposed superhighway would be a monster, with high-speed lanes and freight rail lines, plus pipelines, water, fiber optics and electric power, with gasoline and food concessions, stores, hotels and emergency services in the median.

Suspicions and Answers

Those convinced that the full-bore NAFTA Superhighway is coming point to several disparate efforts that they say prove the government isn't telling the whole truth:

- The controversial effort to build the Trans-Texas Corridor, which would largely parallel existing highways, primarily moving freight. The suspicious see it as the NAFTA Superhighway's first leg.

- A Bush administration proposal to allow some Mexican trucks to drive deeper into the U.S. heartland than previously allowed. A bill to limit the program, proposed by Rep. Nancy Boyda, D-Kan., passed the House, 411-3. (Boyda, a congressional newcomer, defeated a five-term incumbent who had called the superhighway a myth.)

- North America's SuperCorridor Organization, or NASCO. The Texas-based nonprofit coalition advocates for improvements along major trade corridors, such as Interstates 35, 29 and 94.

- The Security and Prosperity Partnership (SPP). It's a collaborative effort on several fronts, including trade and security, by the United States, Canada and Mexico. Critics call it Ground Zero for the push for a North American Union.

Bohigian, the assistant secretary of commerce whose portfolio includes the SPP, said the effort is intended only to "reduce the cost of trade and improve the quality of life" through efforts such as decreasing the wait time for trucks idling at international borders. Reducing the average wait time from 35 minutes to six minutes has saved more than $1 billion, he said.

Fitton of Judicial Watch said much of the activity dates to the establishment on March 23, 2005, of the SPP by Bush, then-Mexican President Vicente Fox and then-Canadian Prime Minister Paul Martin.

Notes obtained from the U.S. government after a meeting in Canada in September 2006 contained the phrase "evolution by stealth," Fitton said.

Sowing the Seeds of Rumor

There's no such thing as a proposed NAFTA Superhighway.

Though opposition to the nonexistent highway is the cause célèbre of many a paranoiac, the myth upon which it rests was not fabricated out of whole cloth. Rather, it has been sewn together from scraps of fact.

Take, for instance, North America's SuperCorridor Organization (NASCO), a trinational coalition of businesses and state and local transportation agencies that, in its own words, focuses "on maximizing the efficiency of our existing transportation infrastructure to support international trade." . . .

A few years ago NASCO put on its home page a map of the United States. . . . Drawn in bright blue, the trade route begins in Monterrey, Mexico, runs up I-35 and branches out after Kansas City, along I-29 toward Winnipeg and I-94 toward Detroit and Toronto. The colorful, cartoonlike image seemed to show right out in the open just where NASCO and its confederates planned to build the NAFTA Superhighway. It began zipping around the Internet. . . .

Ever since the map went live, NASCO has spent a considerable amount of time attempting to refute charges like those made by right-wing nationalist Jerome Corsi, whose recent book *The Late Great USA* devotes several pages to excoriating NASCO for being part of the vanguard of the highway and the coming North American Union.

Christopher Hayes, Nation, *August 27, 2007.*

Matt Englehart, spokesman for the Commerce Department's International Trade Administration, said the North American partnership "is absolutely not a precursor" to a loss of American sovereignty.

"It's about smart and secure borders, promoting the safe and efficient movement of legitimate people and goods," Englehart said.

He described the work by the three governments as "standard intergovernmental diplomacy and coordination that occurs all the time on various issues."

What About That Highway?

The federal government has no plans for a superhighway, Englehart said, but "there are private and state-level interests" pushing something similar. "They describe themselves as NAFTA corridors, but they're not federally driven initiatives, and they're not part of the Security and Prosperity Partnership."

Michael Barkun, a Syracuse University political scientist who specializes in conspiracy theories, said a major theme long has been "that schemes are being hatched to destroy American sovereignty."

"The only thing that's new here is that it appears in the guise of a North American Union," he said. "Previously it appeared in the guise of U.N. domination. I think whatever appeal this has may derive from the fact that there are pre-existing concerns about trade that have been around since the creation of NAFTA, and even more strongly the immigration issue in the sense of border security. So in a way it becomes an issue onto which all kinds of anxieties and concerns can be projected."

Doug Thomas, professor of communications, technology and culture at the University of Southern California, said the advent of the Internet has made conspiracy theories widely available.

"It's the speed and the distribution," he said. "People are able to join in and flush them out a little quicker, so everybody can add a piece to the puzzle."

Periodical Bibliography

The following articles have been selected to supplement the diverse views presented in this chapter.

Piotr C. Brzezinski
"If No One Flies, No One Dies," *Harvard Crimson*, April 20, 2007.

Patrick J. Buchanan
"NAFTA Superhighway: Highroad to National Oblivion?" *VDARE.com*, August 29, 2006.

James Jay Carafano and Alane Kochems
"Security and the Sale of Port Facilities: Facts and Recommendations," Heritage Foundation Web Memo, February 22, 2006. www.heritage.org.

Stephen E. Flynn and James M. Loy
"A Port in the Storm over Dubai," *New York Times*, February 28, 2006.

Christopher Hayes
"The NAFTA Superhighway," *Nation*, August 27, 2007.

Tiffany Melvin
"Here Are the Facts About NASCO; Trade, Transportation Group Not Working on a 'NAFTA Superhighway' Through U.S.," *Salina (KS) Journal*, September 14, 2006.

New York Times
"Our Porous Port Protections," March 10, 2006.

Peggy Noonan
"If Cattle Flew," *Wall Street Journal*, June 3, 2007.

Ron Paul
"The NAFTA Superhighway," *US Fed News Service, Including US State News*, October 30, 2006.

Bruce Schneier
"U.S. Ports Raise Proxy Problem," *Wired*, February 23, 2006.

Patrick Smith
"Is Airport Security Futile?" *Salon.com*, August 17, 2006.

Kelly Taylor
"Taking the High Road," John Birch Society, June 11, 2005, www.jbs.org/node/4134.

OPPOSING
VIEWPOINTS®
SERIES

CHAPTER 3

What Laws Best Protect Driver Safety?

Chapter Preface

Motor vehicle crashes are the leading cause of death for American teens. Indeed, fatal automobile accidents account for 36 percent of all teen deaths. In response to these tragic numbers, policy makers have implemented several strategies to reduce the risks. For example, many states have developed a graduated driver's licensing (GDL) program that imposes restrictions on new drivers during several stages. Some states limit nighttime driving and the number of passengers a teen driver may carry. The most controversial proposal is to increase the driving age to eighteen or even nineteen years. Supporters claim that increasing the driving age would reduce what many see as an epidemic of fatal teen driving accidents. Opponents claim that increasing the driving age is unfair and unnecessary.

Those who believe that the driving age should be increased claim that sixteen-year-olds are simply too immature to drive a vehicle. Research evidence reveals, for example, that a sixteen-year-old brain is not completely developed. When teens are speeding, brain researchers maintain, their brain's thrill center is working perfectly, but the part of their brain that weighs risks is not yet fully developed. "Studies have convinced a growing number of safety experts that sixteen-year-olds are too young to drive safely without supervision," journalist Robert Davis asserts. While graduated licensing and other restrictions have reduced the death toll, teens continue to die in fatal crashes at alarming rates. As a result, public opinion in America increasingly favors raising the driving age. According to Davis, "Among the general public, majorities in both suburbs (65%) and urban areas (60%) favor licensing ages above 16."

Opponents argue that calls to raise the driving age are an overreaction to misleading statistics. Of the approximately 4 million sixteen-year-olds in 2003, only 31 percent were licensed. During that same year, 937 sixteen-year-olds were killed in crashes. Preventing all sixteen-year-olds from driving due to the tragic deaths of such a small minority is, in the view of opponents, unfair. Moreover, raising the driving age would negatively impact the substantial majority of safe sixteen-year-old drivers. Allen Robinson, CEO of the American Driver and Traffic Safety Education Association (ADTSEA), argues that it seems unreasonable "to prevent 1,262,899 sixteen-year-olds from obtaining a drivers license that will assist them with opportunities to: go to school, participate in extracurricular school activities, go to work and be involved in other social activities." Rather than raise the driving age, opponents assert, the more logical solution is to enforce current restrictions and better train all teens to drive safely. "The solution is not preventing licensed use," Robinson reasons, "but to better train and use stricter licensing tests before issuing a drivers license to a sixteen-year-old or any new driver."

The best strategies to reduce teen driving deaths, like many debates over what laws best protect driver safety, remain controversial. The authors in the following chapter debate the efficacy of other driver safety laws.

> "The single greatest defense against highway fatalities is a vehicle's seat belts."

Seat Belts Reduce Highway Fatalities

Danielle E. Roeber

The single most effective way to prevent injury and death on the highway is to wear a seat belt, argues Danielle E. Roeber in the following viewpoint. Since stronger seat belt laws increase seat belt use, she reasons, stronger seat belt laws will in turn save lives. The strongest seat belt laws are primary enforcement laws, in which police officers are authorized to stop and cite unbelted motorists without needing another reason to stop them. Roeber asserts that such laws will increase seat belt use and therefore reduce the economic and human cost of highway accidents. Roeber is the alcohol safety and occupant protection coordinator at the National Transportation Safety Board.

As you read, consider the following questions:

1. According to Roeber, what percentage of ejected passenger-vehicle occupants were killed in 2005?

Danielle E. Roeber, alcohol safety and occupant protection coordinator, National Transportation Safety Board before the Transportation Committee, New Hampshire House of Representatives, on House Bill 802, Seat Belt Legislation, Concord, New Hampshire, March 20, 2007.

2. What is the estimated cost of each critically injured survivor of a motor vehicle crash, according to NHTSA, as cited by Roeber?

3. In the author's opinion, how does seat belt use in primary and secondary enforcement states differ?

The National Transportation Safety Board is an independent Federal agency charged by Congress to investigate transportation accidents, determine their probable cause, and make recommendations to prevent their recurrence. The recommendations that arise from our investigations and safety studies are our most important product. The Safety Board cannot mandate implementation of these recommendations. However, in our 39-year history, organizations and government bodies have adopted more than 80 percent of our recommendations.

The Safety Board has recognized for many years that motor vehicle crashes are responsible for more deaths than crashes in all other transportation modes combined. Every year, more than 90 percent of all transportation-related deaths are caused by highway crashes. The single greatest defense against highway fatalities is a vehicle's seat belts. When used properly, seat belts reduce the risk of fatal injury to front seat vehicle occupants by 45 percent.

Strong Laws Increase Use

Seat belt laws are instrumental to increasing seat belt use, and the stronger the law, the greater the use. Seat belt use in the United States remains considerably lower than use in other industrialized nations precisely because other countries have stronger seat belt laws, and New Hampshire, with no adult seat belt law, has the lowest belt use in the country.

For more than 15 years, the Safety Board has recommended that States enact seat belt laws and authorize primary enforcement of those laws. The Board maintains a Most

Wanted list of safety recommendations because of their potential to save lives. Primary enforcement is one of the issues on that list, the one with the potential to save more lives than any other on the list. It has the potential to save more lives than probably any other piece of legislation you will consider this year.

Today I want to discuss four elements that support the Safety Board's recommendation on primary enforcement seat belt laws. First, seat belts are effective in reducing motor vehicle injuries and fatalities. Second, motor vehicle occupants who do not use seat belts engage more frequently in high-risk behavior. Third, the economic cost from the failure to use seat belts is substantial. Finally, primary enforcement seat belt laws do increase seat belt use.

Seat Belts Are Effective

Seat belts are the number one defense against motor vehicle injuries and fatalities. Seat belts restrain vehicle occupants from the extreme forces experienced during motor vehicle crashes. Unbelted vehicle occupants frequently injure other occupants, and unbelted drivers are less likely than belted drivers to be able to control their vehicles. Also, seat belts prevent occupant ejections. Only 1 percent of vehicle occupants using seat belts are ejected, while 30 percent of unrestrained vehicle occupants are ejected. In 2005, 75 percent of passenger vehicle occupants who were totally ejected from a vehicle were killed.

The National Highway Traffic Safety Administration (NHTSA) estimates that from 1975 through 2005, seat belts saved more than 211,000 lives nationwide. According to NHTSA, had all passenger vehicle occupants over age 4 used seat belts in 2005, an additional 5,300 lives would have been saved. Unfortunately, some motor vehicle occupants mistakenly believe that they are safer without a seat belt, that their vehicle and/or their air bag provides sufficient occupant protection, or that they will not be in a motor vehicle crash where seat belts would make a difference.

Unbelted Drivers and High-Risk Behavior

Approximately 19 percent of motor vehicle occupants nationwide do not use seat belts. These drivers, who choose not to buckle up, tend to exhibit multiple high-risk behaviors and are more frequently involved in crashes. According to the National Automotive Sampling System (crash data composed of representative, randomly selected cases from police reports), belt use among motorists is lowest in the most severe crashes.

Fatal crashes are the most violent motor vehicle crashes and can result from high-risk behaviors such as speeding and impaired driving. Unfortunately, people who engage in these high-risk behaviors also tend not to use their seat belts. While observational surveys have identified an 81 percent seat belt use rate, use in fatal crashes is significantly lower. From 1996 through 2005, almost 840,000 vehicle occupants were involved in fatal crashes. Of those 840,000 occupants, more than 320,000 died. More than 55 percent of the vehicle occupants who died were unrestrained. In New Hampshire, for the same time period, more than 1,000 vehicle occupants died, and almost 65 percent were unrestrained.

Impaired drivers and teen drivers are also considered high-risk drivers. Seat belt use for these populations is substantially lower than the national observed belt use rate. In 2005, only 28 percent of fatally injured drivers who were violating their State's per se impaired driving statute (had a blood alcohol concentration at or above 0.08 percent) were using seat belts. As for teen drivers, researchers found that while belt use was low in States that authorize primary enforcement (47 percent), it was even lower in States with only secondary enforcement seat belt laws (30 percent).

The Effects of Strengthening Safety Belt Laws

State	Passenger vehicle driver deaths 1996–2003	Lives that could have been saved since 1996
Alaska	326	23
Arizona	3,347	234
Arkansas	2,914	204
Colorado	2,646	185
Florida	10,889	761
Idaho	1,158	81
Kansas	2,373	166
Kentucky	4,027	282
Maine	838	59
Massachusetts	1,776	124
Minnesota	2,771	194
Mississippi	4,314	302
Missouri	5,459	382
Montana	1,070	75
Nebraska	1,345	94
Nevada	1,226	89
North Dakota	465	33
Ohio	6,309	441
Pennsylvania	6,644	465
Rhode Island	336	23
South Carolina	4,436	310
South Dakota	699	49
Utah	1,216	85
Vermont	372	26
Virginia	4,200	294
West Virginia	1,759	123
Wisconsin	3,454	242
Wyoming	675	47
Total	**77,084**	**5,390**

Note: States listed are all those with secondary belt laws.

TAKEN FROM: Insurance Institute for Highway Safety, January 27, 2005.

The Economic Costs

Although opponents to primary enforcement seat belt laws claim that nonuse is a personal choice and affects only the individual, the fact is that motor vehicle injuries and fatalities have a significant societal cost. For example, NHTSA calculated that the lifetime cost to society for each fatality is over $977,000, over 80 percent of which is attributed to lost workplace and household productivity. In 2005, more than 5,300 lives and billions of dollars might have been saved if everyone had used a seat belt.

NHTSA estimates that each critically injured survivor of a motor vehicle crash costs an average of $1.1 million. Medical expenses and lost productivity account for 84 percent of the cost of the most serious level of non-fatal injury. In a 1996 study, NHTSA found that the average inpatient cost for unbelted crash victims was 55 percent higher than for belted crash victims. In 2000 alone, seat belts might have prevented more than 142,000 injuries.

While the affected individual covers some of these costs, those not directly involved in crashes pay for nearly three-quarters of all crash costs, primarily through insurance premiums, taxes, and travel delay. In 2000, those not directly involved in crashes paid an estimated $170 billion for crashes that occurred that year; $21 billion, or 9 percent of total economic costs, were borne by public sources (federal and State government). Motor vehicle injuries and deaths experienced by unbelted vehicle occupants cost the Nation's taxpayers an estimated $26 billion just for medical care, lost productivity, and other injury related costs.

Primary Enforcement

Primary enforcement seat belt laws remain the best way to raise and maintain high seat belt use rates. With primary enforcement, police officers are authorized to execute a traffic stop and cite unbelted vehicle occupants without needing another reason for making the stop. According to the National Occupant Protection Usage Survey (June 2006), seat belt use in primary enforcement law States was 85 percent, while the belt use rate in secondary enforcement law States was only 74 percent. States that recently enacted primary enforcement seat belt laws have experienced increased seat belt use rates ranging from almost 5 to almost 18 percentage points. The increased use is based on the perceived risk of being stopped.

Key provisions of a comprehensive seat belt law should also include coverage of all vehicle occupants in all seating positions, coverage of all vehicles, and sufficient penalties to promote compliance with the law.

American citizens support primary enforcement. NHTSA conducted a survey in 2003 to determine the public's opinion on primary enforcement seat belt laws. Overall, 64 percent of the population surveyed supported primary enforcement. Among people from States with secondary enforcement seat belt laws, more than half (56 percent) approved of primary enforcement. Minority populations are strong proponents of primary enforcement. For example, 74 percent of Hispanics surveyed and 67 percent of African Americans surveyed endorsed primary enforcement, as opposed to 62 percent of whites. Traffic crashes affect people of all ethnic backgrounds.

> *"Regulators should take a deep breath, allow beltless motorists to put themselves at risk, and go hassle the dangerous drivers."*

Seat Belt Laws Are Unnecessary

Ted Balaker

Driving laws should protect careful drivers from dangerous drivers, argues Ted Balaker in the following viewpoint. Driving laws should not protect the careless from themselves, he maintains. Those who do not wear seat belts do not put the lives of others at risk, only their own, Balaker asserts. In fact, he reasons, seat belt laws distract the police from their proper role—protecting law-abiding people from those who pose a threat. Balaker is a fellow at the Reason Foundation, a libertarian think tank.

As you read, consider the following questions:

1. How does the Click It or Ticket campaign differ from other campaigns, in Balaker's opinion?

2. In the author's view, what is even more tragic than the death of someone who refuses to wear a seatbelt?

3. According to the author, what are some of the unintended consequences of seat belt laws?

Who's the bigger threat to your safety, a murderer or someone who attempts suicide? The answer is obvious, and we'd certainly jeer any mayor who suggested lowering a city's death toll by cracking down on suicides. Yet something strange happens when death comes to the highway. Politicians lock arms with law enforcement, and come up with campaigns like "Click It or Ticket [CIOT]," which ... aims to reduce highway fatalities through stricter seatbelt law enforcement. Suddenly, the murder-suicide distinction vanishes, and it's perfectly acceptable to reduce deaths by punishing those who put only themselves at risk.

Like other do-gooder efforts that plead with us to turn off our TVs or put down our cigarettes, Click It or Ticket rolls around once every year. But unlike many other campaigns, CIOT doesn't stop with pleading. Cops from over 12,000 law enforcement agencies scope out violators, set up checkpoints and mete out fines as high as $200. In order to emphasize the seriousness of their intentions, they've even adopted the hallmark of all ham-fisted safety crusades—zero tolerance. As one police chief put it: "America should be on notice—Click It or Ticket. No exceptions. No excuses. No warnings."

Protecting the Careless

But why waste cops' time with seatbelt laws? After all, laws shouldn't protect careless people from themselves, they should protect the peaceful from the dangerous. CIOT supporters figure that since so many people die because they refuse to wear seatbelts, the government could save many lives by strapping them in with laws. The implicit rationale is that all of [2003]'s 43,220 highway deaths were equally tragic.

But if an adult does something risky—like tightrope walking, smoking or driving without a seatbelt—that person alone

Click It or Ticket Hysteria

The problem with Click It or Ticket's seat belt hysteria is not just that it distracts law enforcement from its proper highway safety role, targeting drunk and reckless driving, nor the credibility government loses when it seeks to punish people for behavior that puts only themselves at risk. . . .

Of course wearing a seat belt doesn't defend against traffic crashes, only your chances of surviving it. Yet as a simple matter of priorities, we should be willing to differentiate between someone who dies because he wasn't wearing a seat belt and someone who dies as a result of someone else's reckless driving. . . . Public policy should not concern itself with decreasing all highway deaths, but with decreasing the deaths of innocents. A distinction the Click It or Ticket zealots can't seem to make.

Mike Krause, Independence Institute, June 9, 2004.

is responsible for the consequences. And since drivers who don't buckle up aren't making anyone else less safe, laws that bear down on these people don't make other motorists any safer either. We should be allowed to ruin our own lives, but we shouldn't be allowed to ruin the lives of others. So, yes, it's tragic when someone dies because he refused to wear a seatbelt, but it's much more tragic when a reckless driver kills innocent people. Public policy should not concern itself with decreasing all highway deaths, but with decreasing the deaths of innocents.

The Proper Role of Law Enforcement

Even though fans of individual liberty often (and rightly) decry the paternalism embedded in seatbelt laws, most Americans take little offense at such state-sponsored nannying. However, nannying does not just make us less free; when it distracts law enforcement from its proper role, it can also make us less safe. When government assumes many duties, it's tougher to do the important ones right.

Government officials are more on the mark when they call for enforcement of drunk driving laws. But here again law should focus on recklessness, whether it's encouraged by alcohol, fatigue, general stupidity or high-speed lipstick application.

Forty-nine states have seatbelt laws, and in many cases, the laws allow officers to pull over motorists whose only crime is not wearing a seatbelt. While the officer takes time to give the seatbelt scofflaw a scolding and a ticket, plenty of other drivers embark on the kind of harebrained maneuvering that often ends with a reckless driver colliding into a good driver. It's these red-light-running, left-turn-at-any-cost daredevils who enrage and endanger good drivers.

And seatbelt laws come with their own set of unintended consequences, which further complicates the principle that policy should protect the peaceful people from the dangerous. Seatbelt laws may make drivers and children safer, but economists such as Christopher Garbacz suggest that greater safety can make drivers more comfortable with dangerous driving, which puts the lives of more innocents—like pedestrians, cyclists and other passengers—in jeopardy. Risk assessment researchers have long pondered this paradox, and some have even suggested (only half jokingly) that the best way to promote cautious driving would be to attach a twelve-inch buck knife to all steering wheels.

Mandating Safety

Of course, the government's crusade to convert the unbuckled does not stop with seatbelt laws. For decades, mandates have forced automakers to take up the cause. At one point, interlocks actually prevented drivers from starting their cars if their seatbelts weren't snapped on. Public outrage spurred Congress to outlaw such mandates, but the crusade continued.

Today government-mandated lights, chimes and text messages hector drivers when they turn the ignition, and often all the ringing and flashing doesn't stop when the car starts. In many models, chime and light seatbelt reminders can persist for up to five minutes, and safety pushers have even decided to take another stab at interlocks. A proposal before Congress would up the agitation ante by mandating "entertainment interlocks," where drivers could listen to the stereo only if they buckled up.

The good news is that most of us do buckle up. About 80 percent of Americans use seatbelts, a decision probably based less on government nagging than on a simple understanding of the safety benefits. After all, the word is out—seatbelts make you safer. We get it. Why wage an ever-intensifying campaign against the remaining holdouts?

Perhaps one day regulators will understand that—even when armed with all the facts—some people will still choose risky behavior. Instead of saving us from ourselves, regulators should take a deep breath, allow beltless motorists to put themselves at risk, and go hassle the dangerous drivers.

> "In the absence of mandatory motor-
> cycle helmet laws, preventable deaths
> and great suffering will continue to oc-
> cur."

Motorcycle Helmet Laws Save Lives

Marian Moser Jones and Ronald Bayer

*Before the mid-1970s, forty-seven states had mandatory motor-
cycle helmet laws, state Marian Moser Jones and Ronald Bayer
in the following viewpoint. Since the repeal of many such laws,
death and serious injury has increased substantially, the authors
claim. Despite evidence that helmet laws reduce fatalities and severe injuries, however, motorcyclists continue to lobby for helmet
law repeal, the authors assert. Since motorcyclists are clearly un-
able to make sound safety decisions, the authors reason, mandatory helmet laws are necessary. Jones and Bayer are with the
Center for History and Ethics of Public Health at Columbia
University in New York.*

As you read, consider the following questions:

1. According to Jones and Bayer, what constitutional challenges have been made against motorcycle helmet laws?

Marian Moser Jones and Ronald Bayer, "Paternalism & Its Discontents," *American Journal of Public Health*, February 2007. Reprinted with permission from the American Public Health Association.

2. In the authors' opinion, what happened in the four years following the 1975 revision of the National Highway Safety Act?

3. What do the authors claim the history of motorcycle helmet laws in the United States illustrates?

In the face of overwhelming epidemiological evidence that motorcycle helmets reduce accident deaths and injuries, state legislatures in the United States have rolled back motorcycle helmet regulations during the past 30 years. From the jaws of public health victory, the states have snatched defeat. There are many ways to account for the historical arc; we focus here on the enduring impact libertarian and antipaternalistic values may have on US public health policy.

[As of February 2006], only 20 states, the District of Columbia, and Puerto Rico require all motorcycle riders to wear helmets. In another 27 states, mandatory helmet laws apply only to minors (aged younger than 18 years or 21 years depending on the state), and 3 states—Colorado, Illinois, and Iowa—have no motorcycle helmet laws. Additionally, 6 of the 27 states with minor-only helmet laws require that adult riders have $10,000 of insurance coverage or that helmets be worn during the first year of riding. This uneven patchwork of state regulations on motorcycle helmet use contrasts dramatically with the picture 30 years ago, when 47 states, the District of Columbia, and Puerto Rico had passed mandatory helmet laws that applied to all riders. The repeal of motorcycle helmet laws has occurred as the United States has moved toward greater statutory regulation of automobile safety. During the past 20 years, every state except New Hampshire has enacted a mandatory seat belt law, and since 1998, the National Highway and Traffic Safety Administration (NHTSA) has required that all new cars sold in the United States be equipped with dual air bags.

The repeal of motorcycle helmet laws in the United States contradicts a global movement toward enacting mandatory helmet laws; as of 2003, at least 29 countries—including most European Union countries, the Russian Federation, Iceland, and Israel—had passed mandatory helmet laws for motorcycles. Developing countries, including Thailand and Nepal, also have passed helmet laws in recent years. Varying levels of enforcement and other factors, such as the general safety and quality of the roads, influence the effectiveness of these laws in different countries. In 1991, the World Health Organization launched a global helmet initiative to encourage motorcycle and bicycle helmet usage worldwide. . . .

Constitutional Challenges

As soon as states began to pass mandatory helmet laws, opponents mounted constitutional challenges to them. Some challenges involved appeals in criminal cases against motorcyclists who had been arrested for failing to wear helmets; others were civil suits brought by motorcyclists who alleged that the laws deprived them of their rights. Between 1968 and 1970, high courts in Colorado, Hawaii, Louisiana, Missouri, Massachusetts, New Jersey, North Carolina, North Dakota, Ohio, Oregon, Tennessee, Texas, Vermont, Washington, and Wisconsin and lower courts in New York all rejected challenges to the constitutionality of their state motorcycle helmet laws. In June 1972, a US District Court in Massachusetts similarly rejected a challenge to the state's helmet law that was brought on federal constitutional grounds, and in November of that year, the US Supreme Court affirmed this decision on appeal without opinion.

The constitutional challenges focused principally on 2 arguments: (1) helmet statutes violated the equal protection clause of the Fourteenth Amendment or state constitutional equivalents by discriminating against motorcycle riders as a class, and (2) helmet statutes constituted an infringement on the motorcyclists' liberty and an excessive use of the state's police power under the due process clause of the Fourteenth

Amendment or similar state provisions. Only the Illinois Supreme Court and the Michigan Appeals Court accepted these arguments. The Illinois Supreme Court ruled that the helmet laws constituted an infringement on motorcyclists' rights. . . .

The Biker Lobby

Motorcyclists had long been organized—whether they belonged to informal clubs, racing associations under the aegis of the American Motorcycle Association, or "outlaw" biker gangs, such as the Hells Angels—and the passage of motorcycle helmet laws galvanized the groups to become political. During the 1970s, the American Motorcycle Association, which was founded in 1924 as a hobbyist group, organized a lobbying arm to ". . . coordinate national legal activity against unconstitutional and discriminatory laws against motorcyclists, to serve as a sentinel on federal and state legislation affecting motorcyclists, and to be instrumental as a lobbying force for motorcyclists and motorcycling interests." Additionally, those who identified with the biker culture, including members of outlaw motorcycle gangs and thousands of other men who rode choppers (modified motorcycles with high handlebars and custom detailing), became involved in state-level and national level groups that advocated the repeal of helmet laws and other limitations to riding motorcycles. . . .

Other state-level groups, which called themselves motorcyclists' rights organizations, also began to form around the country. The Modified Motorcycle Association, a group of chopper riders founded in 1973 that eschewed the outlaw behavior of Hells Angels, engaged in both antihelmet law political activity and local campaigns against police harassment of bikers.

In 1975, these groups began to turn the tide against proponents of mandatory helmet laws. Motorcyclists, who had only thus far been successful in the appellate courts of 2 states and in stopping helmet bills in California, had evolved into an

organized and powerful national lobby. In June and again in September 1975, hundreds of bikers descended on Washington, DC, where they rode their choppers around the US Capitol to protest mandatory helmet laws. In the post-Watergate environment, motorcyclists found a newly receptive ear in Congress. Representatives of ABATE [American Brotherhood Against Totalitarian Enactments], the American Motorcycle Association, the Modified Motorcycle Association, and other motorcyclists' rights organizations were invited to hearings held in July 1975 by the House Committee on Public Works and Transportation to discuss revisions to the National Highway Safety Act. . . .

Not surprisingly, the issue of choice emerged as the central theme in the arguments of those opposed to helmet laws, similar to the arguments of women's reproductive rights advocates. Just as proponents of legalized abortion had argued that they were not pro-abortion but were in favor of a woman's right to choose whether to terminate a pregnancy, ABATE chapter literature stated "ABATE does not advocate that you ride without a helmet when the law is repealed, only that you have the right to decide."

At the end of the hearings, Representatives James Howard (D-NJ) and Bud Schuster (R-PA) said they would support revisions to the National Highway Safety Act that removed the tie between federal funding and state helmet laws. . . .

The prospect of ending a threat to withdraw highway funds attracted the notice of liberal Senator Alan Cranston (D-CA), who signed on as a cosponsor of a Senate bill introduced by archconservative Senators Jesse Helms (R-NC) and James Abourezk (R-SD). On December 13, 1975, the Senate voted 52 to 37 to approve a bill that revised the National Highway Safety Act. The House passed a similar measure. The revisions were incorporated into a massive $17.5 billion bill for increasing highway funds to the states, and the bill was signed by President Gerald Ford on May 5, 1976.

An Unplanned Public Health Experiment

During the next 4 years, 28 states repealed their mandatory helmet laws. The consequences of these repeals were most succinctly expressed in the September 7, 1978, *Chicago Tribune* headline "Laws Eased, Cycle Deaths Soar." Overall, deaths from motorcycle accidents increased 20%, from 3312 in 1976 to 4062 in 1977. In 1978, NHTSA administrator Joan Claybrook wrote to the governors of states that had repealed their laws and urged them to reinstate the enactments. She cited studies that showed motorcycle fatalities were 3 to 9 times as high among helmetless riders compared with helmeted riders and that head injury rates had increased steeply in states where helmet laws had been repealed. "Now that some states have repealed such legislation we have control and experimental groups which when compared show that one of the rights enhanced by repeal is the right to die in motorcycle deaths," opined an editorialist in the June 1979 issue of the *North Carolina Medical Journal.* . . .

During the next decade, evidence of the human and social costs of repeal continued to mount. Medical costs among helmetless riders increased 200% compared with helmeted riders, and in some states, helmetless riders were more likely to be uninsured. The April 1987 issue of *Texas Medicine* published an editorial entitled "How many deaths will it take?" The editorial exemplified the growing frustration among physicians, epidemiologists, and public health officials with legislatures that failed to act on evidence that showed helmet law repeals increased fatalities and serious injuries. "I invite our legislators and those opposed to helmet laws to spend a few nights in our busy emergency rooms," wrote the author, who was the chief of neurosurgery at Ben Taub General Hospital in Houston. "Let them talk to a few devastated mothers and fathers of sons with severe head injuries—many of whom will needlessly die or remain severely disabled." Posing a challenge to the antipaternalism that had inspired the repeal of laws, he contended, "[a] civilized society makes laws not only to protect a person from his fellowman, but also sometimes from himself as well."

Other studies adopted a more narrowly economic perspective on the impact of helmet law repeals. In a 1983 article, researchers sponsored by the Insurance Institute for Highway Safety used mathematical models to estimate the number of excess deaths—those that would not have occurred had the motorcyclist been wearing a helmet—in the 28 states that had repealed their helmet laws by 1980. They then conducted an economic analysis of the costs to society as a result of these deaths. This cost calculation incorporated direct costs (emergency services, hospital and medical expenses, legal and funeral expenses, and insurance and government administrative costs) and indirect costs (the value of the lost earnings and services due to the death of the person). The researchers found that the costs totaled at least $176.6 million.

In Europe, meanwhile, where helmet laws were being enacted for the first time, studies were showing an opposite effect. In Italy, where a compulsory motorcycle helmet law went into effect in 1986, a group of researchers compared the accidents in 1 district (Cagliari) during the 5 months before and the 5 months after the law's enactment. They found a 30% reduction in motorcycle accidents and an overall reduction in head injuries and deaths.

In Congress Once Again

In May 1989, against a backdrop of 34 states' adoption of mandatory automobile seat belt laws, Senator John Chafee (R-RI) held a news conference to announce he was introducing a bill—the National Highway Fatality and Injury Reduction Act of 1989—that would empower the US Department of Transportation to withhold up to 10% of federal highway aid from any state that did not require motorcyclists to wear helmets and front-seat automobile passengers to wear seat belts. The conference was strategically held during a meeting of the American Trauma Society.

A hearing on the bill that was held by the Senate Committee on Environment and Public Works in October 1989 provided yet one more opportunity to engage (in a federal forum) the argument about the potential benefits that would result from the enactment of mandatory helmet laws and the deep philosophical issues such laws raised. As had others before him, Senator Daniel Patrick Moynihan (D-NY) sought to compare the imposition of helmet requirements with the public health justification for compulsory immunization. Senator James Jeffords (R-VT) responded with an invocation of the antipaternalistic argument so resonant in American political culture. . . .

Instead of confronting the moral arguments made by opponents of helmet laws, proponents of such measures sought once again to marshal the compelling force of evidence. In 1991, at the request of Senator Moynihan, the General Accounting Office issued a comprehensive report that documented the toll. The report reviewed 46 studies and found that they overwhelmingly showed helmet use rose and fatalities and serious injuries plummeted after enactment of mandatory universal helmet laws.

Despite the fierce opposition of motorcycle groups, Senator Chafee ultimately succeeded in getting the motorcycle helmet law and seat belt law provisions added to a major highway funding bill that was passed in December 1991. Under the law—which was far less punitive than what Senator Chafee had originally proposed—states that failed to pass helmet laws would have 3% of their highway funds withheld.

Reenactment and Repeal

In 1991, the momentum seemed to be turning in favor of state motorcycle helmet laws. For the first time in its history, California enacted a universal mandatory helmet law, which took effect on January 1, 1992; however, this brief moment of public health optimism was short-lived. In 1995, after the "Gingrich Revolution," in which conservative Republicans took control of Congress, the national motorcycle lobby succeeded in getting the federal 3% highway safety fund penalties repealed. In 1997, after pressure from state-level motorcycle activists, Arkansas and Texas repealed their universal helmet laws and instead required helmets only for riders aged younger than 21 years. These repeals were followed by similar actions in Kentucky (1998), Louisiana (1999), Florida (2000), and Pennsylvania (2003). In a move that gave credence to the well-worn claim about the social costs of private choice, several of the new laws required riders to have $10,000 of medical insurance coverage policy before they could ride helmetless.

This new round of repeals of motorcycle helmet laws produced a predictable series of studies, with all too predictable results: In Arkansas and Texas, helmet use decreased significantly, head injuries increased, and fatalities rose by 21% and 31%, respectively. In 2003, a study of Louisiana and Kentucky fatalities found that after repeal of helmet laws, there was a 50% increase in fatalities in Kentucky and a 100% increase in fatalities in Louisiana. In 2005, the Insurance Institute for Highway Safety released a study that showed Florida's helmet law repeal had led to a 25% increase in fatalities in 2001 and 2002 compared with the 2 years before the repeal.

Individualism and Public Health

Over the past 30 years, helmet law advocates have gathered a mountain of evidence to support their claims that helmet laws reduce motorcycle accident fatalities and severe injuries. Thanks to the rounds of helmet law repeals, advocates have been able to conclusively prove the converse as well; helmet law repeals increase fatalities and the severity of injuries. But the antihelmet law activists have had 3 decades of experience fighting helmet laws, and they have learned that their strategy of tirelessly lobbying state legislators can work. As one activist wrote, "I learned that the world is run by those who bother to show up to run it." More important, they have learned a lesson about how persuasive unadorned appeals to libertarian values can be.

This history of motorcycle helmet laws in the United States illustrates the profound impact of individualism on American culture and the manner in which this ideological perspective can have a crippling impact on the practice of public health. Although the opponents of motorcycle helmet laws seek to shape evidence to buttress their claims, abundant evidence makes it clear—and has done so for almost 3 decades—that in the absence of mandatory motorcycle helmet laws, preventable deaths and great suffering will continue to occur. The

NHTSA estimated that 10,838 additional lives could have been saved between 1984 and 2004 had all riders and passengers worn helmets. The success of those who oppose such statutes shows the limits of evidence in shaping policy when strongly held ideological commitments are at stake.

Early on in the battles over helmet laws, advocates for mandatory measures placed great stress on the social costs of riding helmetless. The courts, too, have often adopted claims about such costs as they upheld the constitutionality of statutes that impose helmet requirements. Whatever the merit of such a perspective, it clearly involved a transparent attempt to mask the extent to which concerns for the welfare of cyclists themselves were the central motivation for helmet laws. The inability to successfully and consistently defend these measures for what they were—acts of public health paternalism—was an all but fatal limitation.

The recent trend toward motorcycle helmet laws that cover minors, however, shows that legislators and some antihelmet law forces have accepted a role for paternalism in this debate. The need for a law that governs minors shows a tacit acknowledgment that (1) motorcycle helmets reduce deaths and injuries and (2) the state has a role in protecting vulnerable members of society from misjudgments about motorcycle safety. Ironically, then, it is the states within which the motorcycle lobby has been most effective that have most directly engaged paternalist concerns.

The challenge for public health is to expand on this base of justified paternalism and to forthrightly argue in the legislative arena that adults and adolescents need to be protected from their poor judgments about motorcycle helmet use. In doing so, public health officials might well point to the fact that paternalistic protective legislation is part of the warp and woof of public health practice in America. Certainly, a host of legislation—from seat belt laws to increasingly restrictive tobacco measures—is aimed at protecting the people from self-imposed injuries and avoidable harm.

With the latest round of helmet law repeals, motorcycle helmet use has dropped precipitately to 58% nationwide, and fatalities have risen. Need anything more be said to show that motorcyclists have not been able to make sound safety decisions on their own and that mandatory helmet laws are needed to ensure their own safety?

| *"Helmet laws go against the grain of everything this country stands for."*

Motorcycle Helmet Laws Limit Personal Freedom

Jacob Sullum

Many people ride motorcycles because of the feeling of freedom it provides, asserts Jacob Sullum in the following viewpoint. To mandate that motorcyclists wear helmets restricts this personal freedom, he claims. Not only are helmets uncomfortable, Sullum suggests, there is evidence that they increase the rider's risk of injury. Indeed, helmets are much less effective at preventing injuries than seat belts, he maintains. Moreover, he argues, the claim that injuries to helmetless riders are costly for the taxpayer is unwarranted. Sullum is senior editor of Reason, *a libertarian monthly.*

As you read, consider the following questions:

1. What, in Sullum's view, is the Quigley Factor?
2. What did NHTSA report about motorcycle helmets and injuries in its 1996 report, according to the author?
3. In what ways do helmets make accidents more likely, in the author's view?

On a Monday afternoon in June 1999, Richard Quigley was riding his Harley near Capitola, California, when a local police officer pulled him over for violating the state's helmet law. There ensued a half-hour debate with the officer and his supervisor about whether Quigley's headgear—a trucker's cap emblazoned with "United States Freedom Fighter" into which he had inserted a rigid, plastic disc—qualified as a "safety helmet." Quigley, a 61-year-old with a ponytail and a ZZ Top-style beard who directs Bikers of Lesser Tolerance of California and once ran for Congress on the Libertarian ticket, later called the encounter "interesting, informative and fun!"

Richard Quigley's idea of fun, whether riding a motorcycle without a helmet or arguing with the police about it, may not be the same as yours or mine. But his enthusiasm for fighting California's helmet law, a battle in which he has been engaged for seven years "on the streets and in the courts," helps explain a public policy puzzle: While almost every state requires adults to wear seat belts, most do not require them to wear motorcycle helmets, even though riding a motorcycle is much more dangerous than driving a car. The story behind this anomaly is both inspiring and discouraging—inspiring because it shows that a highly motivated minority can make a successful stand for freedom, discouraging because it shows that politics is more important than principle in determining why certain laws aimed at protecting people from their own risky behavior become widely accepted while others remain controversial.

In 2003 there were 5.4 million registered motorcycles in the U.S., compared to about 136 million registered cars. Despite their relatively small numbers, motorcyclists have been far more effective than drivers at resisting traffic safety paternalism. After some initial grumbling, most motorists got used to buckling up and are now unlikely to put up much resistance as states move toward primary enforcement, allowing police to pull people over for not wearing seat belts (as opposed to issuing citations after stopping them for other reasons). By contrast, going back to the 1971 founding of the American Brotherhood Against Totalitarian Enactments (ABATE) by the staff of *Easyriders* magazine, motorcyclists have been willing to invest the time, effort, and money required to fight helmet laws. Call it the Quigley Factor.

Believing in Freedom

"Motorcyclists believe in freedom, and we attack anything that is attacking our freedom," explains Robert Fletcher, coordinator of the Texas ABATE Confederation. "Helmet laws go against the grain of everything this country stands for," says New York Myke, ABATE of California's state director and owner of San Diego Harley Davidson. Just as abortion rights groups insist they do not favor abortion, motorcyclist groups are at pains to make it clear they do not oppose helmets. Jeff Hennie, vice president for government relations at the D.C.-based Motorcycle Riders Foundation, says, "What we're advocating is freedom of choice. . . . It should be the decision of the rider whether to put on extra safety equipment." He describes the attitude of helmet law opponents this way: "Let me decide what is right for me, instead of the government jamming regulations down my throat."

During the last few decades motorcycle activists have been remarkably successful in bringing that message to state legislators and members of Congress. In 1976, responding mainly to state resentment of federal mandates, Congress repealed legislation enacted in 1967 that had made federal highway funds contingent on adoption of helmet laws. At that point every state but California had passed a helmet law (although the Illinois law had been overturned by the state Supreme Court). Freed of the federal requirement, 27 states repealed their helmet laws or limited their coverage to minors (usually meaning riders under 18) during the next few years. Some of those states reinstated helmet requirements for adults in the 1980s and early '90s, including a few that acted after Congress again started tying highway funds to helmet laws in 1991. In 1995, largely in response to lobbying by the Motorcycle Riders Foundation, Congress again eliminated the helmet law mandate, and since then half a dozen states have repealed helmet requirements for adults (one of which, Louisiana, restored universal coverage).

As of July 2005, 30 states still allowed adult motorcyclists the freedom to decide for themselves what, if anything, to wear on their heads. But the insurance industry, safety groups, and the National Highway Traffic Safety Administration (NHTSA) continue to push universal helmet laws, which are periodically introduced by legislators even in states such as Illinois and Minnesota that have long allowed adults to ride without a helmet. Meanwhile, helmet law opponents are lobbying for repeal in California, West Virginia, and elsewhere.

To block or repeal helmet laws, activists must convince legislators to defy public opinion. While a 1978 Louis Harris poll found that 57 percent of Americans thought motorcyclists should be free to ride without helmets, a 2001 survey by the same organization found that 81 percent thought helmets should be required. Add to that the fact that the fatality rate per mile traveled is more than 25 times as high for motorcycles as it is for cars, and the success of helmet law opponents is even more impressive.

The Social Cost Argument

The main argument they've had to counter also plays a conspicuous role in debates over government efforts to discourage risky habits such as smoking, drinking, and overeating. As a 1991 report from the General Accounting Office put it, "society bears the cost, through tax-supported programs as well as insurance premiums, for the additional deaths and serious injuries resulting when motorcycle riders do not use helmets." The courts have almost uniformly approved this alarmingly open-ended rationale for regulation as part of the police power.

Having failed in the courts, helmet law opponents have fended off the "social cost" argument in state legislatures partly by noting that taxpayer expenses associated with injuries that might have been prevented by motorcycle helmets do not amount to much. Although riding a motorcycle is much riskier than driving a car, helmets are considerably less effective at preventing injuries than seat belts are. As NHTSA noted in a 1996 report to Congress, "Helmets cannot protect the rider from most types of injuries." Based on accident data from seven states, NHTSA estimated that motorists involved in crashes who wore seat belts were 20 percent less likely to be injured and 60 percent less likely to be killed than motorists who didn't. The figures for motorcyclists who wore helmets were 9 percent and 35 percent, respectively.

The lower rates are applied to a much smaller population, yielding estimates of lives saved, injuries prevented, and costs avoided that are far less impressive than the ones for seat belts, especially at the state level. NHTSA's numbers indicate that a universal helmet law would prevent about a dozen fatalities a year in Minnesota, for example. As Robert Illingworth of the Minnesota Motorcycle Riders Association bluntly put it in a 1992 interview with the Minneapolis *Star Tribune*, "We're talking about an insignificant amount of money and an insignificant amount of carnage."

"Not-So-Subtle Political Intimidation"

Even these modest projections are open to question. While NHTSA makes much of increased fatalities after states stop forcing adults to wear helmets, some of the additional deaths may be due to increased riding. Helmet law opponents argue that lifting the requirement makes riding more convenient, comfortable, and enjoyable, which encourages current riders to use their bikes more and spurs new registrations, many by motorcyclists who may be more prone to accidents because they are inexperienced or have not ridden in years. . . .

In addition to questioning the effectiveness of helmet laws, motorcycle activists sometimes suggest (in an argument that belies their professed agnosticism on the question of whether it's smart to wear a helmet) that helmets make accidents *more* likely because they increase fatigue and impair hearing, peripheral vision, and awareness of air pressure changes. Once an accident occurs, they argue, the added weight increases the risk of neck and spine injuries. James Baxter, president of the National Motorists Association and a former lobbyist on motorcycle issues, says the arguments suggesting that helmet laws cause injuries "have never been too well documented," but they "provided enough of an excuse for some legislators who wanted to get out from under the issue."

Another important factor that helped helmet law opponents was the decision by motorcycle manufacturers to stay out of the fight. Although a 2004 NHTSA pamphlet lists the Motorcycle Industry Council as a supporter of "universal motorcycle helmet laws," a spokesman for the group, Mike Mount, says it encourages motorcyclists to wear helmets but takes no position on whether they should be legally required to do so. "They are cowed into silence," says Chuck Hurley, executive director of Mothers Against Drunk Driving (MADD), who until [2005] ran the National Safety Council's Air Bag & Seat Belt Safety Campaign. "The most you'll get out of them is that helmets are a good idea."

If motorcycle manufacturers worry about antagonizing their customers, legislators worry about provoking single-issue voters with long memories. The key to resisting motorcycle helmet laws was convincing legislators they would pay at the polls for trying to force helmets onto adults. The laws' opponents did so in ways both dramatic and mundane. They rode into state capitals, thousands at a time, to protest existing laws or forestall new ones. They packed legislative hearing rooms. They met with legislators, wrote letters, and got involved in

The Responsible Adult Rider

Laws mandating helmet use at all times have no significant effect on the safety of motorcycling in general, although they may or may not be beneficial in individual accident circumstances. The decision on when to wear a helmet while operating a motorcycle should remain with each responsible adult rider.

A.B.A.T.E. of Pennsylvania,
Alliance of Bikers Aimed Toward Education, 2007.

party politics. They campaigned for politicians who supported the right to ride without a helmet and against politicians who didn't.

The Minnesota Motorcycle Riders Foundation acquired enough clout to elicit a 1990 pledge from Gov. Arne Carlson to veto any bill extending the state's helmet requirement to adults. A couple of years later, a state legislator who had sponsored an unsuccessful helmet bill complained to the Minneapolis *Star Tribune*: "It's a case of not-so-subtle political intimidation. These [motorcyclists] are people who really feel negatively about something. They are the ones who'll get out and work very hard against you in your district and bad-mouth you."

Each year in Texas, where the legislature freed riders 21 or older from the state's helmet requirement in 1997, Texas ABATE brings several thousand riders in motorcycle attire to the state Capitol in Austin, where they walk the halls, knock on doors, and explain their point of view. Before 2000, when the Florida legislature narrowed the state's helmet law, ABATE of Florida members would ride into Tallahassee bareheaded, with a pre-arranged police escort, and ride out wearing helmets. "It was very orderly," says James "Doc" Reichenbach, the group's president. "This was done very professionally."

The example of Florida, where the helmet requirement for adults was in effect for more than three decades, suggests the importance of another trait: persistence. Opponents of helmet laws across the country "just kept pounding away at this issue," says Baxter. "I think a lot of legislators just felt it wasn't worth the trouble to them personally to get in these people's faces and have them camping on their doorstep, working against them in elections, supporting their opponents." . . .

A Passionate Minority

Why do motorcyclists seem to care so much more about helmet laws than drivers care about seat belt laws, when the underlying principle is the same?

Motorcyclists may have been quicker to recognize the importance of the principle because riding a motorcycle is much more dangerous than most other modes of transportation and forms of recreation. If the government can save lives and taxpayer money by requiring helmets, it could save even more by banning motorcycles altogether. The National Motorists Association's Baxter suggests that motorcyclists' consciousness of their minority status also fed their determination to resist helmet laws. "They knew that if they didn't directly get involved, nobody else was going to," he says.

The way helmet laws are enforced tends to confirm motorcyclists' sense of themselves as a picked-on minority. To begin with, police in states that require adults to use helmets have the authority to stop a motorcyclist simply for failing to wear one, while police in most states still need some other reason to stop a motorist before they can cite him for not buckling up. Even in states with primary seat belt enforcement, a helmetless motorcyclist is more conspicuous than an unbuckled motorist, making him more vulnerable to traffic stops. "The police really don't spot the guy not wearing a seat belt as much as a guy not wearing a helmet," says Texas ABATE's Fletcher. "You can see [the helmetless motorcyclist] three blocks away." Because he cannot credibly attribute his noncompliance to forgetfulness, says Baxter, "a motorcyclist who doesn't wear a helmet is a direct affront to the enforcement community," which makes a stop even likelier and raises the potential for a hostile encounter. And once he is stopped, a motorcyclist may be forced to park his vehicle and walk, unlike an unbelted driver, who can simply buckle up and continue on his way after getting a warning or a ticket.

Another reason helmet laws provoke more resistance than seat belt laws is the comfort factor: While buckling up is relatively painless for most people, wearing a motorcycle helmet that weighs a few pounds and covers most of your head can be tiring and sweaty. "If it's really hot, I absolutely don't wear one," says ABATE of Florida's Reichenbach. "You sit at a stoplight, especially in Florida, you're sitting there in 100 percent humidity, and the sun is beating down on you, and that heat's coming up off the road, which is like 140, 150 degrees. . . . We've had people literally pass out at stoplights wearing helmets."

A Celebration of Freedom

The view of helmets as confining and stifling meshes with the sentiment that forcing people to wear them ruins what is for many riders a visceral experience of freedom. "We're passionate about our motorcycles," says ABATE of California's Myke. "This is something that's more of a way of life than a hobby or a sport. It really goes to the core of our being. . . . Riding a motorcycle is my celebration of freedom." Few motorists feel the same way about driving, which for most of us is a workaday means of getting around, not an important part of our identities.

Hennie, head of the Motorcycle Riders Foundation, says it's hard for the uninitiated to understand how a method of transportation could acquire so much meaning. "If you've never ridden a motorcycle," he says, "there's no way to describe the feeling of freedom. It's got to be the next best thing to being able to fly. When you start putting restrictions on that freedom, people take it personally."

In the final analysis, not enough people took seat belt laws personally. For the most part, whatever objections they harbored were overcome by force of law and force of habit. By contrast, substantial numbers of motorcyclists have complained loudly, conspicuously, and persistently about helmet laws for more than three decades. "Apparently," says the National Safety Council's [director of transportation safety, John] Ulczycki, "legislators are easily convinced that the perceived rights of motorcyclists to injure themselves are more important than the public good." Aside from the tendentious definition of "the public good," this gloss is misleading on two counts: Resistance to helmet laws hasn't been easy, and it hasn't necessarily involved convincing legislators of anything but the motorcyclists' determination. Politicians didn't have to understand their passion to respect it. And therein lies a lesson for the world's busybodies and petty tyrants.

| "The ... use of hand-held cell phones while driving is a public safety hazard that needs to be addressed."

Laws Banning Cell Phone Use While Driving Are Necessary

Joseph J. Hazewski

Holding on to a cell phone while driving endangers public safety, claims Joseph J. Hazewski in the following viewpoint. Driving a motor vehicle safely requires concentration, he argues. Indeed, research conducted by the National Highway Traffic Safety Administration reveals that 80 percent of auto accidents are caused by driver distractions. The states should take a cue from Exxon-Mobil, which forbids its employees to use a cell phone while driving, he concludes. Hazewski is a columnist for the Daily Sun, *the Corsicana, Texas, daily newspaper.*

As you read, consider the following questions:

1. What does Hazewski concede are some of the benefits of a cell phone?

2. What percentage of drivers use cell phones, according to a Nationwide Insurance study, as cited by the author?

Joseph J. Hazewski, "Cell Phones and Driving," *Corsicana Daily Sun*, May 30, 2007. Reproduced by permission.

3. In the author's view, what is the most common action taken by state and local jurisdictions to limit the adverse impact of cell phone use on driving?

How many times a day do you see someone talking on a cell phone while driving? Do you truly believe that individual is focused on their driving? Or more on the conversation? How many close calls (near accidents) have you seen that involved someone who was on a cell phone? Even in Corsicana, with low volume traffic, it is an everyday occurrence.

Cell Phone Close Calls

About a week ago, I was stopped at a traffic signal heading east on Seventh at 24th. A young woman coming down 24th with a cell phone stuck between her ear and her shoulder ran a red light and turned west on Seventh. She turned too wide, almost clipping cars turning left from the turn lane on Seventh. Minutes later I was heading north on Beaton, when a white commercial van with a middle-aged fellow on a cell phone heading west on First Avenue ran the stop sign. Another near miss with a vehicle that had the right-of-way and began entering the intersection. Luckily, the elderly lady driving that vehicle was alert, braked, and avoided a collision.

My favorite multi-tasking driver is one I spotted about a year ago as he passed me on State Highway 31 a couple miles west of Powell. This dexterous individual had a cigarette dangling from his lips, a map unfolded laying across his steering wheel, a beverage in his right hand, and a cell phone crammed between his left ear and shoulder while motoring in excess of 70 mph down the road.

There is no doubt cell phones are extremely useful. Businessmen and women can work on the road. Cell phones offer convenience—check with the home front while out shopping, advise an appointment you are going to be late or early, call a friend just to say, "Hi." Send text messages and pictures. Report an accident or emergency on the road. An unlimited number of uses and a major distraction.

Driving and Cell Phones Do Not Mix

Cell phones may be convenient but there's one place they seem to do more harm than good—and that's behind the steering wheel. Psychological research is showing that when drivers use cell phones, whether hand-held or hands-off, their attention to the road drops and driving skills become even worse than if they had too much to drink. Epidemiological research has found that cell-phone use is associated with a four-fold increase in the odds of getting into an accident—a risk comparable to that of driving with blood alcohol at the legal limit.

American Psychological Association, February 1, 2006.

Driving a motor vehicle is a piece of cake. Everyone does it. The rules of the road are pretty much common sense and easy to follow. But driving is a serious task that if done carelessly in an unfocused manner can kill. More and more states are keeping data on wireless devices and other distractions as contributing factors in motor vehicle accidents.

Cell Phones and Driving Statistics

Recently, I read a 2006 State Legislative Update from the National Conference of State Legislatures (NCSL) entitled "Cell Phones and Highway Safety." Here are some interesting statistics.

The National Highway Traffic Safety Administration (NHTSA), in 2005, reported 43,443 people died and about 2.7 million were injured in 6.16 million police-reported motor vehicle crashes which caused about $230 billion in damages. Nearly 80 percent of the crashes involved some form of driver inattention. That means 4.9 million crashes, 34,000 fatalities, 2.1 million injuries, and $184 billion in damages are the result of driver inattention. It is worth noting a Nationwide Insurance study [that] estimates 73 percent of all drivers use cell phones. A number of public opinion polls have been taken. Gallup found 48 percent of drivers perceive making outgoing calls can make driving dangerous, and 44 percent feel the same about incoming calls. Seventy-one percent of drivers support prohibitions on using hand-held phones while driving. The Farmers Insurance Group confirmed many of the Gallup findings. They also found "87 percent of adults believe using a cell phone impairs a person's ability to drive."

State and local governments have been aware of the high cell phone use and its adverse impact on safe driving for some time. According to NCSL, "During the last five years, lawmakers in every state, Puerto Rico and the District of Columbia (DC) have considered legislation related to cell phone use in cars. Now, 28 have such laws, with more laws likely to pass in 2007."

Cell Phone Prohibitions

Prohibiting the use of hand-held phones while driving is the most common action taken by state and local jurisdictions. California, Connecticut, New Jersey, New York and the D.C. currently prohibit the use of hand-held phones while operating a motor vehicle. They allow hands-free phones in all circumstances. Hand-held phones may be used in emergency only. Using a hand-held phone while driving in all jurisdictions except NJ [New Jersey] is a primary offense for which a motorist can be stopped.

Texas and 12 other states have laws prohibiting novice drivers, those with learner permits, from using cell phones. Although there were a number of bills introduced during [Texas's] 80th Legislative session to impose other restrictions, I do not believe any reached Governor [Rick] Perry's desk.

I don't like big government, and I don't like it when government interferes when it is not needed. However, the obvious public addiction to the use of hand-held cell phones while driving is a public safety hazard that needs to be addressed. . . .

A closing note: Because of potential liability issues, Exxon/Mobil forbids its 88,000 employees from using a cell phone while driving on company business. Many other corporations have done the same, and the Pentagon forbids the use of hand-held phones. Also, more than 40 foreign countries restrict the use of cell phones while driving.

"Mental fitness tests administered yearly after age 70 to keep your driving privileges would ... decrease accidents and fatalities."

Restrictions on Elderly Drivers Are Necessary

Anastasia Niedrich

Mental fitness tests should be administered yearly after age seventy to make America's roads safer, argues Anastasia Niedrich in the following viewpoint. Department of Transportation statistics report that drivers over seventy-five have higher rates of fatal motor vehicle accidents, she notes, and people over seventy-five have the highest rate of pedestrian deaths of any age group. While Niedrich concedes that age should not be the only determining factor in driving fitness, requiring a mental fitness test after age seventy would decrease accidents and fatalities, she maintains. Niedrich is a pre-law student at the University of Utah.

As you read, consider the following questions:

1. What event does Niedrich claim proved her conclusion that there should be maximum age limits for drivers?

Anastasia Niedrich, "Elderly Motorists a Fatal Danger: Drivers Must Be Tested More Often," *Daily Utah Chronicle*, May 31, 2007. Reproduced by permission.

2. What does the author claim will be necessary for mental fitness to be measurable and enforceable?

3. In the author's view, what is one of the skills that would define "mental capacity or fitness"?

I've been saying this for years, and unfortunately, I was proven right with the death of my friend's brother and niece.

On Monday, May 21, 2007, Don and Gwyndalyn Ostler were killed by an 86-year-old man who drove his car into them while they were walking in a crosswalk, attempting to cross the street at 1300 East near 5300 South in Murray, [Utah].

The two were pronounced dead at the scene. Don was 29 years old. Gwyndalyn was five.

There are minimum age restrictions on drivers who—as an age group—are too young to demonstrate the requisite mental fitness to operate a motor vehicle in a manner that is safe for them and other drivers.

Why aren't there maximum age limits for drivers—with that same lack of mental fitness—who are too old to operate a vehicle in that same, safe manner?

Such age limits should exist.

Looking at the Statistics

Before you call me an ageist, consider these facts based on analysis of data from the U.S. Department of Transportation's Fatality Analysis Reporting System: Per mile driven, drivers 75 years and older have higher rates of fatal motor vehicle crashes than drivers in all other age groups except teenagers. People 75 years and older cause the highest rate of pedestrian deaths per 100,000 people of any age group. About 50 percent of fatal crashes involving drivers 80 years and older occur at intersections and involve more than one vehicle. This compares with 23 percent among drivers up to age 50.

Whether an individual is 21 years old or 95 years old, if he or she can't drive safely with the necessary mental fitness and awareness required to not harm other drivers and pedestrians on the road, he or she shouldn't be driving. It's that simple.

For such an assertion to be measurable and enforceable, "mental capacity or fitness" needs to be further defined. But I think all drivers can agree on certain skills and levels of awareness that a person should have in order to safely get behind the wheel.

Tests of Mental Fitness

Mental fitness tests should be administered at regular intervals to keep those who are unfit to drive off the roads—for their safety as well as for ours.

For example, the ability to see and recognize that pedestrians are crossing the street in front of you would be one of the skills someone should have before he or she is allowed to start or continue driving.

Honestly, how many of us were totally safe, capable, aware drivers at age 16, or even at age 18? I know I wasn't. I was involved in an accident the first day I ever drove on my own. I have another family member who was involved in three accidents during the first month he had his license. We were both too young, too inexperienced and I wish that the law had kept us—and others like us—from starting to drive as young as we did.

There should be tougher driving restrictions on all drivers, both young and old. You can argue with assertions like this, but it's hard to argue with government crash statistics.

If you're mentally unfit to drive, you shouldn't be driving. We're all unique individuals. Some of us are not mentally fit to drive until we're age 25 and we lose that mental fitness at age 35, while others are fit to drive safely at age 16 and they maintain that mental fitness until they're 96. For that reason, age should not be the be-all, end-all determining factor for

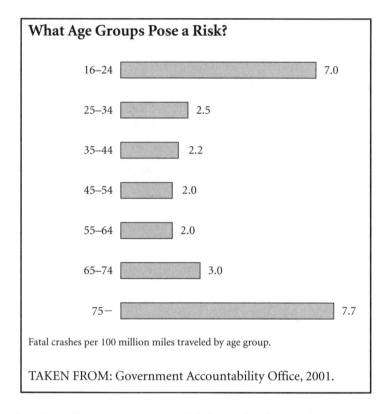

What Age Groups Pose a Risk?

Age Group	Value
16–24	7.0
25–34	2.5
35–44	2.2
45–54	2.0
55–64	2.0
65–74	3.0
75–	7.7

Fatal crashes per 100 million miles traveled by age group.

TAKEN FROM: Government Accountability Office, 2001.

who is allowed to operate a vehicle and who isn't. However, changing the driving age range to 20 to 70 with mental fitness tests administered yearly after age 70 to keep your driving privileges would improve the safe driving situation overall—and decrease accidents and fatalities, according to statistics.

Will such a system be implemented? Likely not.

It's unfortunate that we live in such a reactive society, and it will probably take many more deaths than Don's and Gwyndalyn's, and much more than this article, to change Utah law to prevent mentally unfit drivers from harming or killing others in the future. But if anyone who agrees with my view or cares about this issue is reading this, think about who you want driving around you.

Collectively, we can convey our societal concern about the correlation between age and mental unfitness to drive safely and something productive might actually happen.

It won't bring back Don or Gwyndalyn, but maybe we could save others from death by mentally unfit drivers in the future. I'm sure Don and Gwyndalyn could have only hoped for such a result.

| *"There's no evidence that the elderly make bad drivers."*

Restrictions on Elderly Drivers Are Unnecessary

Eli Lehrer

Drivers between the ages of fifty-five and seventy are safer than drivers in any other age group, claims Eli Lehrer in the following viewpoint. In fact, he maintains, there is no evidence that the elderly are poor drivers. Indeed, Lehrer asserts, companies that profit from safe drivers want to reward elderly drivers because they do not engage in the risky driving behaviors that drivers under twenty-five often do. Driving records and medical conditions should determine driving restrictions, not age, he argues. Lehrer is senior editor of the conservative newsmagazine, the American Enterprise.

As you read, consider the following questions:

1. Why does Lehrer maintain that the statistics about drivers over eighty-five may be skewed?
2. In the author's opinion, what group should face extra hurdles to get a driver's license?

3. According to the author, who gets into more accidents than eighty-five-year-olds?

When George Russell Weller's 1992 Buick LeSabre barreled through a three-block-long farmer's market in downtown Santa Monica [in July 2003,] at least 50 people suffered injuries. At least 10 died and dozens more were injured. Certainly, something went horribly wrong. But, Weller, a mustachioed 88-year-old who walks with a cane and favors golfing attire, hardly seems the sort of person who engages in thrill killing. At worst he behaved in a horribly negligent manner. More likely, some sort of medical or mechanical problem caused his car to get away from him: Witnesses said he was in a trance.

On the tip of many pundits' tongues, however, was a call to make it harder for people Weller's age to get driver's licenses. At least one California newspaper . . . called for tighter licensing requirements for senior citizens and more will surely follow. . . . Far-left former California state senator Tom Hayden pushed for a bill to make it much harder for elderly people to get driver's licenses after a 96-year-old with vision problems mowed down a 16-year-old girl in 1999. Thus, California, along with at least eleven other states, already requires people over 70 (even those with perfect driving records) to renew driver's licenses in person, pass a vision test every year or two, and go through a demeaning street-sign exam.

Examining the Case Against Seniors

But there's no evidence that the elderly make bad drivers. Indeed, nearly all auto-insurance companies reduce rates for drivers over 55. Older people, after all, don't typically drag race, drive aggressively, or get into many accidents. Motorists between 55 and 70 are actually the safest drivers on the road. Only after age 85 do people get into as many accidents as teenagers. Even for this group, the results may be skewed: In most states, motorists don't have to report non-injury accidents. A bump that might rattle a 25-year-old but cause no real injury could break an 85-year-old bone. The absolute number of senior citizens involved in accidents *has* grown significantly (even as auto accidents have fallen elsewhere) but, after adjusting for population growth, numbers of elderly people involved in accidents have remained relatively stable.

The case for making it significantly harder for elderly people to get licenses seems weak in light of the way other drivers get treated. While some states do provide extra tests for people under 18, drivers between 18 and 25 don't face extra hurdles in getting driver's licenses in any state that I could find. If any group should face extra hurdles it's this one: They're such bad drivers that nearly all rental-car and insurance companies charge them extra, while some turn them away altogether. Males 18 to 25, indeed, get into many more accidents than 85-year-olds, overall. Only a few states, likewise, have special rules for 16- and 17-year-old drivers even though they can't rent cars from any well-known car-rental company. Companies that make profits off of safe drivers, in other words, justifiably want to discriminate against teenage drivers but rarely hassle older drivers at all.

No regulation will ever make it perfectly safe for anybody to drive a two-ton hunk of steel at 65-miles-per-hour. Some older motorists, particularly those with health and vision problems, do warrant extra attention from the government, but driving records and diagnosed medical conditions, not age alone, should help policymakers decide who should get off the road. A handful of tragic deaths, in other words, do not justify revoking the driving privileges that millions of seniors depend on.

Periodical Bibliography

The following articles have been selected to supplement the diverse views presented in this chapter.

American
Psychological
Association

"Driven to Distraction," February 1, 2006.

Charles Anderson

"Opposing View: Seniors Are More Cautious," *USA Today*, April 17, 2007.

David J. Houston and
Lilliard E. Richardson

"Safety Belt Use and the Switch to Primary Enforcement, 1991–2003," *American Journal of Public Health*, November 2006.

*Issues & Controversies
On File*

"Drivers' Penchant for Cellular Telephones Cause Problems on U.S. Roads," July 7, 2006.

Kathleen Kingsbury

"Hardheaded?" *Time*, June 26, 2006.

Courtney C. Radsch

"No Talking Behind the Wheel," *New York Times Upfront*, April 18, 2005.

Justin Rinkert

"The Elderly Driver," *Psychiatric Times*, June 2005.

David L. Strayer, Frank
A. Drews, and Dennis
J. Crouch

"A Comparison of the Cell Phone Driver and the Drunk Driver," *Human Factors*, Summer 2006.

William Triplett

"Teen Driving," *CQ Researcher*, January 7, 2005.

Joseph B. White

"Eyes on the Road: Bikers Fight to Ride Free—and Win; Data Show Increase in Fatalities Among Motorcyclists," *Wall Street Journal*, July 30, 2007.

Walter E. Williams

"Buckling Under the Law," *Western Standard*, August 8, 2005.

Tom Zeller

"Is Multitasking a Crime?" *New York Times Upfront*, May 7, 2007.

OPPOSING
VIEWPOINTS®
SERIES

CHAPTER 4

What Is the Future of Transportation?

Chapter Preface

Imagine driving down the street and before you can react, your car automatically slows down because it is communicating with the car ahead of you. Your car learned, long before you, that its driver had slammed on the brakes. Cars that communicate are not science fiction. Indeed, automakers are already testing Vehicle Safety Communication (VSC) technologies. Automakers foresee wireless transponders in vehicles that will transmit ten times per second a vehicle's location, speed, and identity to another vehicle, to a traffic signal—indeed to any receiver programmed to read the message. While most agree that such technology has significant benefits, some see potential dangers that must be addressed before VSC technology becomes widespread.

Few commentators dispute the advantages of VSC technology: VSC would increase driver awareness, improve safety, and relieve traffic congestion. In addition to slowing a car in response to a braking vehicle ahead, VSC will also notify drivers that fast-moving cars are entering a vehicle's blind spot or warn of an impending collision at a traffic signal. In the event of a collision, VSC will deploy air bags more quickly than in current vehicles. VSC will also notify drivers approaching traffic jams and recommend alternate routes. VSC "may even enable high-speed 'platooning' of groups of vehicles on the freeway ... which could help keep our burgeoning population of commuters moving freely," claims *Motor Trend* magazine writer Frank Markus. VSC is also more economical than current systems. According to Markus, VSC will replace about $2000 worth of radar, sonar, and laser sensors on today's vehicles with $100 worth of software, a global positioning system antenna, and a two-way radio.

Despite these advantages, many analysts recommend caution. Widespread and immediate broadcast of information about a driver's identity and location raises concerns about both security and privacy. Michael Zimmer, of Yale Law School, who studies the societal impact of technology, argues that those who send the information must "ensure that no one hacks into the system to pretend to be a car, pretend to be an emergency vehicle, or otherwise disrupt the system, which would compromise its goals for highway safety." Privacy concerns also loom large in the eyes of VSC critics. Since transmitters will likely take the place of license plates, instead of visually broadcasting license numbers to those in close proximity, VSC technology can broadcast information about an individual's identity and location over a much greater distance. Zimmer maintains, "VSC technologies will be constantly transmitting information about identity, location and status for reception by other vehicles, roadside infrastructure, or anyone else with the proper receiving equipment." While people have the reasonable expectation that they may be observed by others in close proximity, they may not expect the widespread distribution of their identity that VSC technology will provide. These observers argue that before widespread implementation of VSC technology, automakers and policy makers must clarify who will have access to the data transmitted, to what extent, and for how long. Zimmer concludes, "Since VSC will have substantial effects on the lives of virtually everyone, it would be most desirable to have broad public participation in the processes that are defining the technology."

The future of VSC technology is uncertain. The authors in the following chapter explore the benefits and challenges of other transportation technologies that may affect the future of transportation.

| "Magnetic levitation is the rail industry's
rising star."

Maglev Trains Have
Significant Benefits

Eric Russell

Interest in magnetic levitation, or maglev, trains is growing, claims Eric Russell in the following viewpoint. Maglev trains use magnetic forces to float and pull trains along a monorail-like track. Because there is no mechanical contact, Russell reasons, maglev trains require less maintenance and make less noise. Moreover, he asserts, the expense of maglev trains will soon be overcome by newer, simpler designs. High speeds and low energy costs make maglev trains a desirable alternative to traditional railways, he maintains. Russell writes for Engineer Live, *a British online engineering magazine.*

As you read, consider the following questions:

1. According to Russell, who was the father of the linear motor?

2. In the author's opinion, why is the maglev train ideal for urban environments?

Eric Russell, "Maglev: Does Magnetic Power Point the Way Forward for Railway Industry?" *Engineer Live*, 2005, www.engineerlive.com. Reproduced by permission.

3. How does the Transrapid maglev system differ from other maglev systems, in the author's view?

Magnetic levitation is the rail industry's rising star just now. But it has been a long time coming. It was in 1947 that the UK's [United Kingdom's] Professor Eric Laithwaite was first called the father of the linear motor, the concept behind maglev. He opened out an electric motor to 'create a magnetic river capable of providing friction-free travel,' as he told 1950s television audiences. Today, more maglev systems are being designed and built than ever before.

How Maglev Trains Work

In a rail system, the linear motor is like a conventional electric motor with its stator cut open and stretched out over the length of the guideway. Instead of a magnetic rotary field, the current in the windings generates a magnetic field of travelling waves, which pulls the vehicle without contact.

By changing the intensity and frequency of the driving current, speed and thrust can be continuously adjusted. When the motor is operated as a generator, the direction of the energy flow is reversed and used for contactless braking.

On inclines, the windings can be installed closer together to provide greater pulling and braking power. In addition, only that section of the linear motor on which the vehicle moves is powered. This prevents two vehicles from being in the same section at the same time.

One method of levitation uses arrays of permanent magnets mounted on the train. These induce strong repulsing currents in a track made up of coils, pushing up on the cars magnetically and levitating them. Alternatively, electromagnets can be located on each side of the train. These are magnetically attracted upwards to iron rails positioned under the edges of the guideway structure. The magnetic force then lifts the vehicle.

The train must be balanced on the magnetic field against varying passenger loads, wind buffeting and centrifugal effects on bends. This requires very accurate and fast control, which is easier to implement with today's electronic systems.

The Benefits of Maglev Trains

Because there is no mechanical contact between guideway and train, there is no mechanical noise and no friction to overcome. This reduces the amount of maintenance needed. It also means that maglev is ideal for urban environments. There is no need for underground tunnels to cut down noise, for example. Trains can also run in all weathers, on steep inclines and in tight turns.

Critics say maglev is a high cost system, but proponents say that costs are comparable with new motorways. But Tony Morris, president of American Maglev Technology, says his design costs much less than motorways, as will be shown in a maglev system under construction at Old Dominion University in Norfolk, Virginia. It features an elevated guideway that runs above the sidewalk.

Also in the USA, scientists at Lawrence Livermore University have developed a new approach to magnetically levitating high-speed trains. Richard Post, team leader, says the design is much simpler in design and operation, potentially much less expensive and more widely adaptable than other maglev systems. Called Inductrack, the system employs special arrays of permanent magnets that induce strong repulsing currents in a track made up of coils, pushing up on the cars and levitating them. It has been successfully demonstrated in test trials and could soon be implemented in Pennsylvania.

Inductrack comprises an array of permanent magnets, active at room temperature, mounted on the train and a track embedded with close-packed coils of insulated copper wire. The permanent magnets are arranged in configurations called

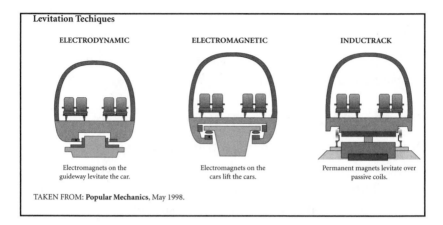

Levitation Techiques

ELECTRODYNAMIC | ELECTROMAGNETIC | INDUCTRACK

Electromagnets on the guideway levitate the car.

Electromagnets on the cars lift the cars.

Permanent magnets levitate over passive coils.

TAKEN FROM: **Popular Mechanics**, May 1998.

Halbach arrays, originally conceived for particle accelerators. They concentrate the magnetic field on one side while cancelling it on the opposite side.

When mounted on the bottom of a rail car, the arrays generate a magnetic field that induces currents in the track coils below the moving car, lifting the car by several centimetres and stabilising it in the centre of the guideway.

Using Auxiliary Wheels

When the train car is at rest, as in a station, no levitation occurs, and the car is supported by auxiliary wheels. Once the train exceeds a transitional speed of 1 to 2km [kilometres] an hour, which is achieved by means of a low-energy auxiliary power source, the arrays induce sufficient currents in the track's inductive coils to levitate the train.

Even though the electromagnetic drag associated with Inductrack becomes small at high speeds, Post says an auxiliary power source would also be needed to maintain the train's high speed against aerodynamic drag.

The theory predicts levitation forces of up to 50 metric tons per square metre of magnet array using modern permanent magnet materials such as neodymium-iron-boron. The theory also shows levitation of loads approaching 50 times the weight of the magnets, important for reducing the cost relative to maglev vehicles.

If the external drive power ever fails, or when the train arrives at a station, the train simply coasts to a stop, easing down on its auxiliary wheels, making it a fail-safe system.

The Halbach array offers other benefits besides levitation. Because its magnetic fields cancel out above the magnets, there is no worry about magnetic fields affecting passengers' heart pacemakers. In contrast, passengers must be magnetically shielded on maglev trains employing superconducting coils. Post says the consulting company of Booz-Allen and Hamilton conducted a preliminary feasibility study of Inductrack and compared it to other maglev technologies. The study found that while an Inductrack system would cost more to build than conventional rail systems, it should be less expensive than maglev trains using superconducting coils. The study also found that Inductrack should be able to achieve speeds of 350km [217 miles] per hour [kph] while offering lower energy costs, noise and propulsion maintenance.

An Alternative Technique

A different type of maglev system, termed Transrapid, is presently operating in Germany. Instead of using superconducting magnets on the maglev vehicle, it uses conventional, room temperature electromagnets. These are located on each side of the vehicle, and run along its entire length. They are magnetically attracted upwards to iron rails positioned under the edges of the guideway structure. The magnetic lift force then levitates the vehicle.

Since the attractive force between the vehicle electromagnets and the iron rails on the guideway increases as the gap between them decreases, the Transrapid Levitation system maintains stability by servo control of the current that energises the magnets. Upward movements of the vehicle are countered by decreasing the magnet current, while downwards movements from the rails increase the magnet current.

So, rather than relying on the passive stability inherent in the superconducting maglev system, where any small displacement from the equilibrium suspension point is automatically countered by an induced magnetic force in the guideway, the Transrapid system relies on active stabilisation to maintain levitation of the maglev vehicles.

The gap between the vehicle and the guideway is continuously monitored, and the current in the electromagnets continuously adjusted on a time scale of thousandths of a second.

The magnitude of the gap is small, about 10mm [millimetres]. In comparison, superconducting maglev operates with a larger vehicle to guideway gap, typically of the order of 100–150mm. The large gap allows the tolerances for construction of superconducting maglev guideways to be greater. This means lower guideway cost and reduced sensitivity to earth settling and thermal expansion effects.

Transrapid has demonstrated safe and reliable operation of its maglev vehicles at speeds up to 450kph [280 mph] on its 35km test track in Emsland, Germany, on which it has now carried hundreds of thousands of passengers. The system has been certified as ready for commercial service.

> "Maglev is a nifty technology but . . .
> such systems are spectacularly expen-
> sive."

Maglev Trains Are Impractical and Expensive

Los Angeles Times

According to the editors of the Los Angeles Times *in the follow-ing viewpoint, maglev (magnetic levitation) trains, which use magnetic forces to float and pull trains along a monorail-like track, are much too expensive to be practical. Indeed, they main-tain, the enormous cost of maglev trains has prevented proposals to link major cities in California from becoming a reality. One proposed maglev route would connect Las Vegas to Primm, Ne-vada, an isolated development that boasts nothing more than an outlet mall and a roller coaster. Taxpayers, they reason, should not have to pay for a train, even a high-tech one, that goes no-where.*

As you read, consider the following questions:

1. To what do the editors of the *Los Angeles Times* attribute the zeal of maglev supporters?

2. In the authors' opinion, what do some estimate is the cost per mile to construct a maglev train?

3. To what do the authors attribute the fact that the Primm line is a candidate for federal maglev train funding?

"Magnetic levitation." The phrase evokes both spirituality and science fiction, like transcendental meditation mixed with supersonic transportation. Perhaps that explains the almost messianic zeal of its supporters, who think it is the public transit savior come to deliver us from clattering trains and lead us not into gridlock.

The long-running debate over "maglev" trains is a battle between faith and reason. Converts believe magnetic levitation—which uses magnetic force to lift cars just above the tracks, allowing speeds of more than 300 mph—is one of the greatest inventions since the wheel. They have to rely on faith because there is very little evidence of the practicality of these systems. [As of May 2005,] only one commercial high-speed maglev train exists, covering a 19-mile stretch from Shanghai to Pudong International Airport [in China].

Arguing from reason are those who concede that maglev is a nifty technology but recognize that such systems are spectacularly expensive—$80 million a mile to construct, by some estimates. Why spend so much money, especially if it's from taxpayers, when you might get more bang for the buck out of cheaper alternatives?

California has spent millions studying a bullet train from San Diego to Sacramento, a proposal that has languished for 12 years. The Southern California Assn. of Governments has proposed a maglev system to connect the region's airports. But it's indicative of the visionary, if slightly off-kilter, nature of maglev supporters that the least practical proposal in the West may now have the best chance to become reality.

An Impractical Proposal

A federal transportation bill that includes funding for maglev has passed in the House and awaits a vote in the Senate. There are three finalists for $950 million, one of which is a 40-mile hop from Las Vegas to Primm, Nev., on the California border. Primm is the home of an outlet mall and a big roller coaster. Beyond that, there's no there there.

The Vegas-to-Primm route is envisioned as the first leg of a system that would eventually run all the way to Anaheim. But for that to happen, California would have to agree to build the rest of the line—and the state already rejected that idea more than a decade ago. Las Vegas boosters somehow managed to keep a straight face while claiming that the Vegas-to-Primm line would make $50 million in annual profits. Ask the folks at Amtrak whether trains that go from somewhere to nowhere make that kind of money.

That the Primm line has gotten this far is a tribute to the power and determination of the Senate minority leader, Harry Reid of Nevada, who undoubtedly sees maglev as promising a new transportation system for pork. Maglev is an interesting technology that bears watching, especially if ways can be found to reduce the cost. But there is no urgent need for a bullet train from Sin City to Disneyland, let alone to Primm.

> *"While seemingly drawn from a science-fiction author's imagination, researchers are actually hard at work developing the 'space elevator,' as a cheaper, more efficient alternative to rockets."*

Space Elevators Will Transport People and Payloads Into Space

Keith Gerein

Unlike expensive rocket boosters, space elevators can cheaply transport people and cargo into space. The space elevator would consist of a tether or ribbon powered with lasers on earth linked to a satellite traveling the same speed as earth, explains Keith Gerein. People and payloads could then be hoisted using mechanical methods at a fraction of the cost of rocket power. Gerein is a writer for the Edmonton Journal *in Alberta, Canada.*

As you read, consider the following questions:

1. According to Gerein, in how many years could the space elevator be an achievable goal?

2. What does the author say scientists are currently considering using as an alternative to steel for the space elevator?

3. What are the alternative sources to laser power being worked on by University of Alberta students, according to Gerein?

At first glance, the idea appears ludicrous. An elevator that doesn't stop at the penthouse, but instead continues skyward along a cable no thicker than a sheet of paper. When it finally stops, its passengers are in orbit around Earth, some 35,000 kilometres [21,748 miles] above the surface.

While seemingly drawn from a science-fiction author's imagination, researchers are actually hard at work developing the "space elevator" as a cheaper, more efficient alternative to rockets.

[In the fall of 2007], teams of engineering students, including one from the University of Alberta [U of A], hope to contribute to the project by entering their devices in a prestigious NASA [National Aeronautics and Space Administration]-sponsored competition.

Elevators as the New Space Shuttles

"It's a really far-out idea, but also realistic because it could be achieved within the next 20 years or so," said Chris Ryziuk, an electrical engineering student who is part of the U of A team. "It could entirely change how we view space travel. Space shuttles aren't very efficient, so this elevator concept may have a big impact on what we can do."

The commonly accepted vision of the space elevator begins with an ocean-based platform built near the Earth's equator. From the platform, a super-strong tether or ribbon would rise into space, attached at the far end to a counterweight located beyond the planet's geosynchronous orbit. In theory, the ribbon will remain taut due to the constant rotation of the

Earth—similar to the round-the-world yo-yo trick in which the string stays tight as the toy is whipped around in a circle.

Elevators or "crawlers" powered by laser beams would then climb up and down the ribbon, transporting humans, supplies and science equipment to space stations or spacecraft. Some scientists estimate each device could lift up to 180 tonnes of material at a cost of $100 per kilogram, much cheaper than the $10,000-per-kilogram cost offered by rockets.

The biggest problem for scholars is the design of the ribbon, which must be extremely strong, but also light enough that it doesn't collapse under its own weight, said Abdulhakem Elezzabi, the U of A team's supervisor.

Realistic Expectations

Currently, scientists are looking at using carbon nanotubes—an arrangement of carbon atoms—that are up to a hundred times stronger than steel, but only one-fifth the weight. Using this material, a suitable ribbon could be designed that is about a metre wide and as thick as a sheet of paper. The challenge will be finding a way to fuse together enough nanotubes to create a tether that is up to 100,000 kilometres long, Elezzabi said. At the NASA competition, teams are being asked to build a small, less powerful version of the elevator.

[In 2006], organizers wanted a device capable of rising 60 metres [66 yards] at a rate of one metre per second. No one met the requirements, although a team from the University of Saskatchewan came close.

For [2007]'s event, set for Oct. 19-21 in Salt Lake City, the difficulty has doubled—120 metres [131 yards] at a speed of two metres per second.

The Goal of Victory

Ryziuk believes his U of A team has a good shot at winning the $500,000 top prize, but acknowledges they will face some tough competition. He said his team is subsisting on a budget

Taking the First Steps

If you can make it into low-Earth orbit—about 160 kilometers [100 miles] up—then you are halfway to anywhere in the solar system. Sci-fi writer Robert Heinlein's remark has become a mantra in the space community, mainly for its irony: despite leaps in rocket technology costing billions of dollars, those first 160 kilometers are still the hardest.

Now . . . a handful of entrepreneurs are going all out to crack the problem. Their solution is a device that is almost the complete opposite of the brute-force approach so long embodied by the crackling power of the rocket engine. They want to step into a small airtight box, push a button marked "space", and ride an elevator all the way up a cable reaching far into the sky.

Even the most optimistic admit that a functional space elevator is still at least decade away. Yet the idea has been gathering momentum since 1999 when a NASA [National Aeronautics and Space Administration] study claimed that an elevator was feasible. [In 2006] US company LiftPort successfully unrolled a 1.6-kilometre-long [1-mile-long] carbon ribbon in the skies above Arizona, stretched it taut using helium-filled balloons and sent a robotic climber scrambling up part of its length. The company aims to build a functioning space elevator by 2018.

Greg Klerkx, New Scientist,
September 2–8, 2006.

of about $10,000 in donations from the university, while other teams, such as the Massachusetts Institute of Technology, are rumoured to have up to $50,000 US.

"We can't buy our way to victory, but a good design goes a long way," Ryziuk said.

Teammate Sebastian Hanula said the largest headache has been designing the power system, especially when using bits and pieces salvaged from garage sales.

"You have to deliver a substantial amount of power and do it safely in a way that doesn't melt the crawler."

Working with small budgets, most teams can't afford lasers so they have to rely on other energy sources. In the past, big lights, engines or heating devices have been used to generate the needed energy for the crawler, Ryziuk said. To maintain secrecy, he declined to reveal what technology the U of A is employing.

Ryziuk and Hanula both hope their work can help advance the project to the point where real space elevators can be built in their lifetime. While the science of the concept is sound, problems will come from the politics surrounding it, Ryziuk said. "Who will fund it? Who will own it? Who will protect it? Who will get to use it?"

"As so often when waiting for a lift, there is now likely to be a long wait until [the space elevator] arrives."

Space Elevator Development Faces Serious Challenges

The Economist

The companies pursuing the space elevator must overcome serious hurdles before the technology will be able to transport payloads or people into space, maintain the editors of the Economist, *a British newsmagazine. Although the concept of the space elevator is simple—a cable runs from Earth to a satellite traveling the same speed as Earth—finding a cable both strong and light enough has been more difficult, the authors claim. Powering the elevator and dodging space debris, the authors assert, are additional challenges space elevator companies must overcome before the space elevator becomes a reality.*

As you read, consider the following questions:

1. According to the *Economist*, who was the first person to suggest the idea of a space elevator?

2. How long would the cable to the space elevator satellite be, according to the authors?

3. In the authors' view, what must be overcome for nanotubes to serve as a space elevator cable?

For decades science-fiction writers and engineers have
dreamed of building a lift [elevator] from the Earth's surface into space. Konstantin Tsiolkovsky, a Russian scientist,
suggested a similar idea more than a century ago, and in 1979
Arthur C. Clarke wrote an entire novel, "The Fountains of
Paradise", about the construction of a space elevator. Whisking
satellites, space probes and even people into orbit on a giant
elevator appears far more civilised than expensive, unreliable
rockets.

Now this fanciful dream is taking its first tentative steps
towards reality. Two companies, LiftPort and X-Tech Projects,
have been founded to pursue commercial space-elevator
projects, and America's space agency, NASA [National Aeronautics and Space Administration] has provided a $400,000
prize-fund for an annual competition, the Space Elevator
Challenge, to encourage space-elevator research. At [the 2006]
contest, . . . 21 teams test[ed] their designs for cables, and robotic lifts to climb up them.

The Challenges

The concept of a space elevator is simple enough. An orbiting
satellite is linked to the surface of the Earth by a cable, which
vehicles then climb up and down. However, to reach a satellite
in geostationary orbit;—which takes exactly a day to circle the
Earth, and so seems to hover above a single spot on the equator—the cable would have to be nearly 35,800km (22,250
miles) long. Such a cable would have to be phenomenally
strong and light to support its own weight.

It has long been recognised that carbon nanotubes, tiny
molecular-scale threads of carbon atoms, would be strong
enough to build such a cable. (Even though nanotubes were
discovered only in 1991, Dr Clarke suggested something very

Predicting Transportation Technology

Transportation landmarks . . . will help pave the way for the more significant innovations.

- By 2010 personal transportation devices will be all the rage and electric shoes with built-in roller-skates will be gaining much of the attention. After nine years of heavy media coverage, the Segway Human Transporter will begin to gain serious market share.

- By 2015 traditional gas-powered autos will start to decline with electric automobiles and hybrids taking up most of the slack.

- By 2020 we will see an industry being built up around self-illuminating highways—highways that glow in the dark. "Glow Roads" will dramatically change the night-time aesthetics of major cities and will be shown to improve driving safety at night and reduce the need for streetlights.

- By 2025 a first attempt at launching the space elevator will fail, setting the industry back a decade.

Thomas Frey,
Da Vinci Institute, 2007.

similar in his book: a "hyperfilament" made of "pseudo-one-dimensional diamond crystal.") But it is not yet possible to produce nanotubes in sufficient quantity, or to knit them into a rope with anything like the strength of the tiny, individual tubes. So far, the strongest commercially available fibre of the required weight is around 4% as strong as a space elevator would require, says Ben Shelef, co-founder of the Spaceward Foundation, which runs the space-elevator competition. He notes that if researchers can increase the strength of that fibre by 50% a year, they will produce a fibre strong enough by 2013. Such speedy progress is not unusual in a new field.

The next problem is to work out how to power the lifts, which will take several days to make the long trip into orbit. Carrying fuel or batteries on board would be impractical, as this would add massively to the weight of the lift, and reduce its carrying capacity. So both LiftPort and X-Tech are designing climbing modules equipped with solar panels that receive power from a laser beamed from the ground. The technology to make this possible is still under development, but compared with the challenges posed by the cable, it's straightforward, says Mr Shelef.

Then there is the danger of orbiting space debris left over from decades of launches, which could damage or destroy the cable. Mr Shelef proposes using radar to detect chunks of debris before a collision, and then steering the cable around them. Fixing the bottom of the cable to an ocean-going platform would make it easy to move, he suggests.

A Long Wait

If these problems can be overcome, building a space elevator is expected to cost around $10 billion—a modest sum by the standards of space exploration. LiftPort estimates that satellites could be launched at around one thousandth of the cost of using rockets. But NASA is sceptical, despite supporting the space-elevator competition. "Since the basic material has yet to be developed, it is still in the research phase and is not a current programme at NASA," says a spokesman.

In February [2006] LiftPort conducted one of the most elaborate space-elevator tests so far. Hot-air balloons secured a cable in place for six hours, and robots then climbed up and down it. The cable reached only a mile into the sky, it is true. But engineers have, in effect, pressed the "call" button—though as so often when waiting for a lift, there is now likely to be a long wait until it arrives.

> *"Scads of private suborbital space vehicles will be popping up all over the planet and breaking out of Earth's atmosphere."*

Commercial Space Travel Will Become Increasingly Common

Katherine Mangu-Ward

The government's monopoly over space is coming to an end, claims Katherine Mangu-Ward in the following viewpoint. Tech millionaires are filling the gap and have set their sights on private space travel, she reports. Private space travel companies will first take tourists on suborbital tours—about sixty-two miles above sea level, she explains. However, she asserts, space entrepreneurs plan to expand the industry to the moon and beyond. While the first space tourists will be adventurers, space entrepreneurs ultimately hope to gain a broad range of consumers, she notes. Mangu-Ward is an associate editor for Reason *magazine.*

As you read, consider the following questions:

1. In Mangu-Ward's opinion, who is the biggest name in the NewSpace business?

Katherine Mangu-Ward, "Space Travel for Fun and Profit: The Private Space Industry Soars Higher by Lowering Its Sights," *Reason*, vol. 38, January 2007, p. 38. Copyright 2007 by Reason Foundation, 3415 S. Sepulveda Blvd., Suite 400, Los Angeles, CA 90034, www.reason.com. Reproduced by permission.

2. What does the author claim led to the end of NASA's monopoly on space?

3. How much does the Federal Aviation Administration's Office of Commercial Space Transportation estimate the space industry will be worth in 2026?

Barbed wire surrounded the Bigelow Aerospace compound, set in a stretch of dry, rockstrewn Nevada desert. Las Vegas glittered in the distance, but otherwise the vista had the desolate look of a lunar landscape, with one difference: The summer heat was oppressive—enough to make you long for the cool vacuum of outer space.

The van full of visiting space geeks didn't mind the harsh conditions. They happily left the air-conditioned glamour of Vegas' Flamingo Hotel and Casino, where the cream of the private space industry had gathered for the NewSpace 2006 conference, to spend a few hours at Bigelow's warehouse and mission control center. They couldn't have been more excited if the van had been on its way to a Star Trek–themed strip club.

The Launch of Genesis I

Earlier in the week, Bigelow Aerospace had successfully launched Genesis I into orbit. A small pod that inflates once aloft, Genesis I is a prototype for cheap, livable, interconnecting rooms for commercial use in space. The first in a series of launches scheduled every six months for the next two and a half years, it marked the beginning of what could be the first privately funded space station.

Robert Bigelow, president and CEO of the company, made his fortune with the hotel chain Budget Suites of America and other real estate ventures. He has a logical goal in mind: an orbital hotel. Similar in concept to the International Space Station but much larger, Bigelow's space-habitat project uses a cast-off National Aeronautics and Space Administration

(NASA) system of inflatable pods. He bought the rights to the technology in 2001, when he read that NASA was scrapping the promising system after many years and many more millions of dollars of development. Bigelow, 62, has since sunk $75 million into the project, with a promise of $425 million more to come.

Stepping inside Bigelow Aerospace's cool, antiseptic, heavily guarded warehouse was like walking into a science fiction novel. Enormous models and pieces of space-bound machinery were strewn about like forgotten Lego blocks over tens of thousands of square feet. The delegation from the NewSpace conference shuffled along with the quiet awe usually reserved for holy places. At one point, a member of Bigelow's mission control team looked at his watch and said, "Actually, Genesis should be passing overhead right now." Everyone in the room looked up, instinctively, as though the module would be visible. Then they grinned sheepishly at each other.

The grins reflected something more than embarrassment at having fallen for an old gag. ("Hey look," someone cracked, "gullible is written on the ceiling.") The visitors were just plain happy. After years of hope and speculation, the private-sector space enthusiasts were thrilled to hear the words "It's overhead right now" from one of their own.

Suborbital Vehicles

The Genesis launch, while exciting, is peanuts compared to what's coming. . . . Besides the ever-larger Bigelow launches, scads of private suborbital space vehicles will be popping up all over the planet and breaking out of Earth's atmosphere, about 62 miles above sea level.

Bigelow and his ilk are part of an industry that calls itself NewSpace, though some prefer the techy alt.space and others favor the touchy-feely personal space. Since the late '90s, they've been coalescing into clubs, nonprofits, and other associations. In the bad old days, this crowd got together mostly to bitch about NASA and its evil stepchildren, Lockheed and Boeing. But while NASA remains a topic of interest, NewSpacers have passed out of their whiny adolescent phase and into industrious young adulthood. Their aspirations are appropriately modest—mostly suborbital, just a quick trip to the edge of the atmosphere. They're setting aside deep space exploration and the moon for now (though they talk a big game about what's next), opting instead for reasonable, practical, short-term goals: quick hops for tourists and other near-to-Earth fun. And instead of crying on each other's shoulders, suddenly the NewSpacers are seeing each other—and sometimes NASA—as the competition.

Thanks in part to a preponderance of tech millionaires, the NewSpace industry is picking up speed. As Bigelow has noted, "We are probably a very close cousin to the world of the Internet and the computer world—doubling every 18 months."

In addition to big-name companies like Virgin Galactic, dozens of smaller entrepreneurial ventures wait in the wings, including Armadillo Aerospace, the rocket company started by Doom and Quake programmer John Carmack. So do communications equipment manufacturers, spacesuit designers, and many other enterprises, releasing pent-up innovation and creativity as NASA's long-lived monopoly on space, or at least suborbital space, wheezes to an end.

The industry, dominated just a few years ago by a bunch of seemingly loony space cadets with big dreams, is becoming the province of respectable, hardheaded CEOs. What happened?

Three-Hour Tours

The biggest name in the NewSpace business is the British billionaire Richard Branson. The pop entrepreneur founded the space tourism company Virgin Galactic in 2004, and he plans to be flying missions by 2008. Apparently taking a page from

Gilligan's Island, Virgin will carry paying passengers on three-hour tours, complete with seven minutes of zero gravity, after just a week of preflight training. The Virgin spacecraft will be modeled on SpaceShipOne, the vehicle dreamed up by the aviation legend Burt Rutan. Rutan's spacecraft captured the privately funded Ansari X Prize in 2004 by being the first private manned ship to exit the atmosphere twice in a span of two weeks. After taking the $10 million prize, Rutan's company, Scaled Composites, signed with Branson to build the bigger, better SpaceShipTwo. Rutan says the new ship will fly higher than the first model and carry eight people.

Branson has generated headlines for the private spaceflight industry (and himself) by accepting several $200,000 down payments for early flights. Potential tourist-astronauts include [musician] Moby, [actress] Sigourney Weaver, Brad Pitt, [wheelchair-bound physics genius] Stephen Hawking, and Paris Hilton. In March 2005, Doug Ramsberg of Northglenn, Colorado, won a free trip on a Virgin vehicle in a company-sponsored lottery. (Perhaps he'll be one of the lucky few to witness Hawking and Hilton colliding in a brainy yet glamorous zero-g mishap.) Branson says he intends to be on the first flight of the geekily named VSS Enterprise, along with members of his family, [in early 2009]. . . .

Branson and his peers are confining themselves to suborbital travel for now: blastoff, a few minutes of zero gravity at the edge of space, then back again. The technology to make this type of trip has been around for decades, though NewSpacers are working to make the trip exponentially cheaper, better, and faster. Bigelow's hotel-in-space project is more ambitious, on a par with the International Space Station, but also has a longer time horizon. And no one has taken serious practical steps toward a private voyage to the moon, though there has been a lot of discussion about the legal preconditions to make a moon trip attractive to entrepreneurs. For starters, it's not clear how property rights will work on the moon or on asteroids. Who is allowed to build, and where? Perhaps more important, what can be brought back to Earth and sold?

Devotees of private space travel have long blamed NASA's monopolistic behavior for their own failures. And it's true NASA has done virtually nothing to encourage outside innovation over the years—despite repeated mandates to do so—while selfishly sucking up billions of dollars and all the dreams and hopes of space buffs nationwide. But when the NewSpacers lowered their sights from "infinity and beyond" to a few minutes of floating, they realized NASA couldn't really stop them from snagging a little bit of space all their own.

Extraterrestrial Entrepreneurs

It was 1999 when the free market faction of the space world finally gave up on NASA. In that single year, NASA boasted two failed Mars robot missions, a mostly grounded shuttle fleet, a busted space telescope, and a semi-abandoned space station; it also aborted several pet projects, from a space plane to a planned landing on a comet's nucleus, in large part because they were politically inexpedient. Most space geeks had long ago lost hope that NASA would ever make it back to the moon, as the space agency seemed resigned to sending shuttles scooting back and forth to the International Space Station with small scientific payloads, spare parts, and the occasional astronaut. Pessimists pointed to the average age of NASA professionals, a ripe old 46, and sighed about the lack of innovation. Gone were the Apollo days, when the command was "Waste anything but time." NASA seemed happy to clunk along with its $16 billion a year, doing what it had been doing since the 1970s: not much.

From that despair, the seeds of dozens of companies were tossed to the winds. A few promise bumper crops soon. Once the really big projects were out of the picture—Mars colonies, dinner at the Restaurant at the End of the Universe, etc.—a

The New Space Race

The next space race is underway. The market for commercial space tourism is expected to generate more than $1 billion in annual revenue by 2020. . . . Billionaire entrepreneurs are looking to fill that demand, partnering with governments to build launching pads and training facilities around the globe, and thrill seekers are already lining up to buy tickets. While most of the world's 35 functioning spaceports are controlled by governments, at least eight private ones are in the planning or construction stages, from Singapore to Sweden.

Allan Madrid and Michael Hastings, "The New Space Race,"
Newsweek, *September 18, 2006.*

few guys with big money started to ask: What could be worse than NASA? We might as well try. . . .

Selling Space

The Vegas conference was dubbed NewSpace 2006 but could just as easily have been called "Selling Space," since pretty much everyone in the room was doing just that, in one capacity or another. As one participant noted: "A few years ago, all these guys had the names of struggling nonprofits on their nametags. Today everyone's a CEO."

For years the Space Frontier Foundation, which organized the conference, has been nagging space geeks to stop thinking like engineers and start thinking like businessmen. The trouble with engineers, apparently, is that they are naturally authoritarian. If we could just calculate everything out to the nth decimal place, they say, we could tell you the One Right Way to get to the moon or to launch a rocket. During the no-go '90s, conferences about commercial space ventures were dominated by talk of propellant, rocket design, and lunar habitation specs. "Here's the thing," warns Kevin Greene, founder of a fledgling startup called Lunar Constructors. "There is no 'optimum design' for a moon colony. This is hard for engineers to understand. This is not a libertarian tirade; there is a role for government. But don't over-design it."

Bigelow agrees with the sentiment, adding: "Whether you're building a regional shopping center mall or a 70-story office building, go out and find your anchor tenants. Don't build the whole thing from your idea of what might work."

Having shed their pocket protectors and donned pinstriped suits and silk ties—most of which, mercifully, didn't have little shooting stars or pictures of the starship Enterprise on them—NewSpace enthusiasts have grown comfortable with the language, and the indeterminacies, of business. The conference participants talked about "selling ourselves to the public," market segmentation, and strategies to fend off government regulation. Many were starting to think beyond the One Right Way to get to space and beginning to consider extra frills to offer travelers once they're up there. . . .

The guys pitching wacky projects have one thing right, though: If the public is going to be interested, it needs to see exciting images and hear wild stories about space. Grainy footage of "One small step . . ." can sustain people's interest only for so long. NASA has lost its touch at selling space, and NewSpace companies are just starting to learn the skill. Virgin Galactic has done the best job so far, with a sharp little product placement in the recent Superman movie: A Virgin Galactic–branded spaceship, possibly piloted by Branson himself, appeared in trailers for the film.

Answering Customer Demand

Even without a totally refined message or perfect, snazzy graphics, a handful of wealthy people are ready to get suborbital. The recent, highly publicized trip to the space station by

Anousheh Ansari, the entrepreneur who helped bankroll the X Prize, has kindled broad interest in personal space travel. Another female space-traveler-to-be, Reda Anderson, told NewSpace participants she didn't need more reassurance or sales pitches; she preferred the rugged appeal of the young industry. "We're not tourists here," she said. "We're not going to go up and spend time in a hotel and have a nice meal and all that kind of stuff." The first breed of space tourists and entrepreneurs will be attracted, as one conference participant noted, by the fact that space is "fresh real estate, like the Internet," room to grow and expand in an essentially lawless atmosphere (or, more precisely, no atmosphere at all).

But an industry cannot live off adventurers and libertarian dreams alone. Although the market is largely untested, a 2002 survey by the research group Futron found that interest levels were high enough to generate more than 15,000 suborbital tourists by 2021, assuming the price of a ticket comes down to about $25,000 (in 2006 dollars). The Federal Aviation Administration's Office of Commercial Space Transportation put out a report [in February 2006] estimating the space travel industry would be worth $1 billion a year within 20 years.

The industry is already talking about what's next if and when suborbital jaunts become commonplace. Unlike NASA, commercial space companies answer directly to customer demand, so the dream of pushing on to the moon is strong. "That's what people want—the moon," says Bigelow with a grin. "But we've got a lot of steps before we get there. It doesn't mean we're not always thinking about it, though." . . .

Someone will be able to make money by taking people into space on a privately developed, privately owned spaceship. They won't go very far, and they won't be gone very long. But just a few short years ago, the smartest guys in the room were content to sit around and argue better than anyone else. Now—with help from an infusion of smart, rich guys—they're fighting for success in a competitive industry with real results on the horizon.

> "Not only is NASA developing its own flying cars, but it's also working on a ... navigation system that could make skyways safer than highways."

Flying Cars May Soon Take to the Air

Christopher McDougall

Private entrepreneurs and NASA, the National Aeronautics and Space Administration, are actively pursuing personal air vehicles, asserts Christopher McDougall in the following viewpoint. Easy-to-use automated navigation systems—on board air-traffic controllers—will make flying cars safe, McDougall explains. The primary challenge for flying-car entrepreneurs is raising money, he maintains. However, one entrepreneur, Rafi Yoeli, hopes to sell his CityHawk to governments that see its advantages as a rescue and police vehicle. McDougall writes for Esquire, Men's Health, *and the* New York Times Magazine.

As you read, consider the following questions:

1. According to McDougall, what three generations of cars does NASA plan to develop over the next fifteen years?

2. How long does NASA's Hahn, cited by McDougall, estimate it will take to train people to fly cars?

3. What event prompted Rafi Yoeli to see the use of flying cars differently, according to the author?

The world has never been kind to flying-car dreamers like Henry Smolinski, who died in 1973 when his Ford Pinto with the welded-on Cessna wings crashed; or Paul Moller, who balances work on his multiengine Batmobile with life-extension experiments so he will still be alive when Skycars fill the skies over Los Angeles; or Rafi Yoeli, who built CityHawk in the living room of his second-floor apartment and had to remove a wall to get it out.

Major automakers don't let them through the door, nor do they get any respect from the earthbound drivers they hope to liberate from traffic. Probably the nicest thing anyone has ever called Rafi Yoeli is "Don Quixote"—but it wasn't by the neighbors, who couldn't help hearing the constant hiss and crackle of his all-night welding.

"People like to call us nuts," Paul Moller says. "I don't care. What innovative thinker hasn't been called a nut?" Moller, who has gambled millions of dollars and his 40-year reputation as an ace aerospace engineer on getting Skycar into the air, pauses for a second, then repeats the word with unmistakable pride: "Nut!"

The World of the Future

But that was the world of the past, before a troubled freeway system and new security concerns prompted NASA to start taking the flying-car dreamers more seriously. . . . NASA has quietly shifted some of its attention from space exploration to the space right over our roofs. Not only is NASA developing its own flying cars, but it's also working on a collision-deterring navigation system that could make skyways safer than highways.

"You can say our goal is to make the second car in every driveway a personal air vehicle," says Andrew Hahn, an analyst at NASA's Langley Research Center in Hampton, Va. Hahn's engineers are already committed to a 15-year time line for three successive generations of flying cars. The first will resemble a compact Cessna with folding wings that converts to road use; it should be available as a graduation gift when this year's freshmen class leaves high school [in 2008]. The second, with a rollout planned for 2015, is a two-person pod with small wings and a rear-mounted propeller. The third will rise straight up like a mini-Harrier jet and should be on the market by the time your newborn has a learner's permit. The first of the three vehicles shouldn't cost more than a Mercedes.

An affordable flying car within five years is a dizzyingly fast evolution—for everyone except Yoeli and other do-it-yourself auto pilots. They've been preparing for this future for decades, and unlike NASA, they can't afford to wait much longer.

The Birth of the Aerocar

Ed Sweeney has had the longest and most frustrating wait, because he is one of the few flying-car men who has already been there; thanks to a lucky encounter years ago, he knows firsthand what it feels like to drive a car into the clouds. In 1959, he was a 17-year-old who flew his radio controlled model planes on a small airfield in Longview, Wash. While Sweeney played outside, an inventor and Navy pilot named Moulton (Molt) Taylor tinkered in a hangar nearby.

Inventors have been trying to cross-pollinate cars and planes since the early days of both, but they always ran up against the difficulty of designing a vehicle light enough to achieve lift with a wing that was both small enough to fit on a street and sturdy enough for stormy skies. Miscalculations were often deadly. The ConvAirCar crashed in the desert on its third flight; the Roadable III smashed into the ground, as did Smolinski's airborne Pinto after the wing struts collapsed.

But a planemobile, Taylor reasoned, didn't have to always be both car and plane at the same time. What if the wings and propeller were just accessories that could be put on before takeoff, then removed after landing? You could tow the wings back home, or leave them at the airfield until the next flight. Beginning with a little yellow car that looked like a Mini Cooper, Taylor made a detachable wing-propeller combo that could be bolted snugly onto the back of his car in five minutes.

After several solo test flights, Taylor took Sweeney up for a ride and even let the teenager pilot the car. They reached the end of the runway at a legal driving speed of 55 miles per hour, got lift and kept climbing. After a while, Taylor looked down and decided they had gone high enough. He had Sweeney guide the little yellow car through a few basic maneuvers, then bring it down for a landing. After hitting the runway smoothly, Sweeney braked as if he were parking his car in the driveway.

Selling the Flying Car

Taylor worked to come up with a commercial version of the Aerocar and, according to Sweeney, was eventually on the verge of a deal with Ford in the early 1970's. Apparently the automaker got last-minute jitters about linking its name to what could become an expensive flop and legendary joke and killed the deal. Sweeney was later surprised to find the Aerocar for sale in the classifieds. He bought his old hero's dream and has since become obsessed with applying Taylor's original design to the lighter, more aerodynamic Lotus. . . . Sweeney . . . hopes to finalize a deal with a major aerospace company and have a production model of the Aerocar ready for testing [soon].

The reason Taylor failed, Sweeney came to understand, was that the Aerocar was stuck in a sort of dead zone between two types of potential customers. Pilots didn't want the boxy vehicle because they could get a far zippier plane for the same money; car drivers didn't want it either, because the Aerocar red-lined at 60 miles per hour on the road and couldn't be flown without a pilot's license. And once drivers learn to fly, they become pilots and are right back in category No. 1. To succeed where Taylor failed, Sweeney would have to make his Aerocar fly and drive faster than Taylor had ever planned. And the new generation of do-it-yourself makers of flying cars now actually has a chance of doing just that. Until the recent rise of the Hummers and S.U.V.'s, the guiding principles of late-20th-century auto design were aerodynamics and super-light compound shells. It's almost as if Detroit were drafting its new models with men like Ed Sweeney in mind.

The next crucial step was simplifying the controls. Sweeney would never make the Aerocar fly better than a plane, so he would have to make it elementary enough for the average commuter to master without full pilot's training. Here again, technology is paving the way. With radar, automatic transmissions and Global Positioning System [G.P.S.] navigation, there's no reason a flying car can't be as easy to handle as any VW [Volkswagen], maybe even easier: your car can't help you merge on the freeway, but according to Andrew Hahn of NASA, most flying smart cars will be controlled by a simple joystick and come preprogrammed with anticollision technology and self-correcting flight controls.

The Benefits of Automated Navigation

"We don't want someone to look at the dash panel and say, 'Oh, my God!' and get right out," Hahn says. "With single-lever acceleration, pilots won't have to go through such rigorous training to get accredited." Hahn estimates that training on flying smart cars could be done in five days for about

$1,000—about what it now costs a 15-year-old to complete driver's ed. Automated flight controls will be unnoticed if you do everything perfectly, but they will override an incorrect manual landing plan. "It's like an instructor-pilot backup," Hahn says. "Even if you have a heart attack, the computerized backup will complete the flight for you."

One beneficiary of computerized navigation is national security: thanks to G.P.S. and cellphone technology, flying cars could be tracked more easily than any road vehicle. NASA is already at work on a device that will function as an on-board air-traffic controller, and the agency expects to have it ready in time for the debut of its first flying car, the EQuiPT, or Easy Quiet Personal Transport. (NASA prefers the term "personal air vehicle" to "flying car.") The vehicle will automatically broadcast information on its location, so ground monitors and every other aircraft in the sky will know exactly who and where you are. (Any rogue vehicle ought to be easily spotted; another driver who sees a car that is in the air but not on his monitor can be expected to sound the alarm.)

Automated navigation will also keep airborne drivers from smashing into one another. If the computerized navigation system senses a tree, or another plane, or the White House, it won't let you steer in that direction. "The technology already exists in the military, and we're adapting it so it can come standard on any personal air vehicle and still be affordable," Sally Johnson, the technical leader of NASA's Small Aircraft Transportation System (SATS) project, says. "It's not a big jump to put these on flying cars," adds Johnson, who is in regular communication with Hahn and his EQuiPT team. "We talk to them and make sure that what we're doing dovetails with what they're doing, and we've found the two are very complementary and synergistic."

Taking to the Air

"SATS is what will make flying cars possible," says Yoeli, who started with the simplest flying-car concept of all. His first

The Small Aircraft Transportation System

The four key things the [Small Aircraft Transportation System, or SATS] offers:

1. Automated flight-path management systems that allow higher volume operations at airports that don't have towers or terminal radar.

2. Guidance and display systems to allow pilots to land safely in low-visibility conditions at minimally equipped airports.

3. On-board graphics and data displays to improve single pilot performance.

4. Assessment of the effects of seamlessly integrating a large number of SATS aircraft into the national airspace system.

Jonathan Glancey, Guardian *(UK), June 16, 2005.*

major invention, a flying boogie board he called the Hummingbird, came from the realization that getting lift isn't really hard. Push air down, and up you go. So he built a fan, pointed it at the ground and shot up into the air. To steer, he leaned right or left. The whole thing was so easy to assemble and such a breeze to fly, Yoeli says, that he became nervous about releasing it to the general public. He had planned to make his fortune from it, but when most of the 1,600 people who replied to his first ad sounded like "Jackass" [an extreme stunt TV show and movie]-style daredevils, he decided he had to first find some way to make the Hummingbird safer.

Yoeli figured that he could make a stable, hovering, untippable flying platform by bolting two Hummingbirds together. "I've been involved in vertical takeoff and landing all my life,"

Yoeli says. He was an aerospace engineer in charge of a design team for Israel Aircraft Industries before going to work for Boeing; later he returned to school for a Ph.D. in artificial intelligence. He started his own aerospace consulting company, which built prototypes of unmanned vehicles and helicopters, but once the idea of a flying car came to him, he sold his share in the company to devote himself to it full time.

Yoeli was deep into the construction of CityHawk, which looked a little like an Everglades airboat and a lot like Luke Skywalker's landspeeder, when the terrorist attacks happened on Sept. 11, [2001]. That should have put an end to his flying-car fantasy right there—there was no way anyone was now going to be allowed to drive through the air in a jet-propelled Subaru. And didn't the police have enough trouble without suspects taking wing during a high-speed chase? Just when Yoeli was finally clearing the technological hurdles, his dream of the future had become stuck in a world of the present.

The Law Enforcement and Military Interest

But Yoeli saw things differently, as any man who builds full-size aircraft in a second-floor apartment would. A year before the attacks, and purely by coincidence, Yoeli imagined City-Hawk responding to exactly the kind of downtown disaster he had witnessed on TV on Sept. 11. "Operation close to buildings will be no restriction for the CityHawk, and it will in fact be able to rescue trapped people inside high-rise buildings by hovering close to a window and allowing a person to step on to the platform," he wrote in an April 2000 press release. CityHawk would be a lifesaver, not a menace; from the start, Yoeli had designed it for inner-city police patrols navigating urban canyons. It was precisely because of terrorist threats and the emergence of street-by-street urban warfare that flying cars were now inevitable, Yoeli insisted. He contacted high-ranking American and Israeli military friends and asked if they would be interested in a superfast aircraft with a vertical range from mere inches to 12,000 feet. The response, he says, was a unanimous "How soon can we get it?"

Once Yoeli saw the military interest in CityHawk, he immediately began working on a far more powerful version, the X-Hawk. X-Hawk's propulsion comes from ducted fans, two encased propellers that push air downward. Yoeli's special innovation was installing hundreds of small vanes at both ends of each ducted fan, like the slats of venetian blinds. By adjusting the pitch of the vanes, Yoeli says, X-Hawk can make minute adjustments in any direction and instantly adjust to wind gusts. And unlike a helicopter, he stresses, X-Hawk can hover inches from a building because the propellers are encased.

A Race Against Time

In California, Paul Moller is using similar technology to build his M400 Skycar, which looks like something that might come roaring out of the Bat Cave. Skycar has four seats, an in-flight speed of 350 m.p.h. and a range of 750 miles, and it can fit in any standard parking space. Moller figures the first few M400's will cost about $500,000—and even at that price he claims he has more than 100 customers already lined up. As production increases, he foresees sticker prices eventually dropping below $100,000. The future of Skycar, however, depends on whether he can get F.A.A. [Federal Aviation Administration] certification and keep raising cash; Moller claims it has already cost $100 million, and his attempt to raise more by taking the company public saw the stock almost immediately relegated to pink-sheet status.

Yoeli is also in a race against time. To stay afloat, he needs to start selling X-Hawks within the next few years. But he has one enthusiastic and well-financed partner lined up now. STAT MedEvac, an emergency-rescue company based in Pittsburgh, can't wait to get its hands on the first F.A.A.-approved X-Hawks. "This can be a very profitable investment for us," James Bothwell, the STAT MedEvac C.E.O., says. "When it comes to using helicopters in cities and suburbs, we're extremely limited in the places we can land, so a paramedic unit on the scene would have to transport a victim two or three blocks to meet the chopper." With X-Hawk, Bothwell estimates, his pilots will be able to fly at least 1,000 missions a year that would otherwise be impossible due to weather or ground conditions.

"I'm always a hopeful kind of guy," says Bothwell, who has been in regular contact with Yoeli's design team for the past two years. "By 2010, I can see us having five or six X-Hawks in our fleet." But by then, Yoeli reckons, you may already have one in yours.

Periodical Bibliography

The following articles have been selected to supplement the diverse views presented in this chapter.

Alan S. Brown	"Maglev Goes to Work," *Mechanical Engineering*, June 2006.
Engineer	"Maglev Trains: Pulling Power," January 23, 2004.
Thomas Frey	"2050 and the Future of Transportation," Da Vinci Institute, 2007, www.davinciinstitute.com/page.php?ID=150.
Lee Gomes	"Is the Final Frontier Just One Ride Away on a Space Elevator?" *Wall Street Journal*, August 22, 2007.
Michael Hastings and Allan Madrid	"The New Space Race," *Newsweek*, August 7, 2006.
Jean M. Hoffman	"To Infinity . . . and Beyond!" *Machine Design*, March 8, 2007.
Pierre Home-Douglas	"Top Floor, Please," *ASEE Prism*, Summer 2006.
Greg Klerkx	"Elevator to the Stars," *New Scientist*, September 2–8, 2006.
David Kushner	"Forget Flying Cars. Meet the Drivable Plane," *Business 2.0*, December 2006.
John R. Quain	"Connected Traveler: Riding the Rails to the Future," *PC Magazine*, August 7, 2007.
Douglas Rushkoff	"Driving Used to Be About Taking on the World. Now It's About Being Tucked in for a Nap," *Discover*, April 2007.
Larry Smith	"Where's My Cool Stuff?" *Popular Science*, March 2006.
Cathy Booth Thomas	"The Space Cowboys," *Time*, March 5, 2007.

For Further Discussion

Chapter 1

1. The chapter authors debate the merit of several different alternative transportation strategies. Which strategy do you think will have the greatest impact? Explain, citing from the viewpoints.

2. John Stossel asserts that the only people who benefit from ethanol are corn farmers and those who process ethanol. According to Brian Jennings, the fact that American farmers and local investors produce and profit from ethanol is a reason to support, not oppose, ethanol because it promotes American energy independence. Which argument do you find more persuasive? Do the authors' affiliations affect their arguments' persuasiveness? Explain your answers, citing from the viewpoints.

3. Daniel Sperling and Joan Ogden tout the long-term benefits of hydrogen as an alternative fuel. Joseph J. Romm does not dispute hydrogen's benefits but maintains that the costs will be high and will divert funds from short-term efforts to reduce dangerous fossil fuels. What types of evidence do the authors use to support their claims? Is one type of evidence more persuasive than another? Citing from the viewpoints, explain your answer.

4. To support his argument that most Americans will continue to choose cars over public transportation, Joel Kotkin points out that even when gas prices rise, Americans continue to drive their cars. Lester Hoel, in his viewpoint supporting public transportation, claims that despite the freedom that cars provide, simply building more roads

will not resolve traffic congestion. Each author uses a different type of rhetoric. Which rhetorical strategy do you find more persuasive? Explain.

Chapter 2

1. Anthony Gregory argues that the private sector will best protect airport security. Paul C. Light counters that privatizing airport security will not improve security as both public and private security face the same challenges. Which viewpoint do you find more persuasive? Explain, citing from the viewpoints.

2. Philip Dine argues that NAFTA Superhighway claims are fueled by unwarranted fears of globalization and immigration. Do you think Kelly Taylor's rhetoric feeds these fears? Explain why or why not, citing from the viewpoint.

3. What commonalities among the viewpoints on both sides of the debate can you find in this chapter? Explain, citing from the viewpoints.

Chapter 3

1. Seat belt law supporter Danielle E. Roeber believes that one role of law enforcement is to protect people from their own poor driving decisions. Seat belt law opponent Ted Balaker believes that protecting people from themselves is a waste of resources. The role of law enforcement, he argues, is to protect good drivers from dangerous ones. Which position do you think is more persuasive? Explain, citing from the viewpoints.

2. Anastasia Niedrich and Eli Lehrer both cite elderly drivers' crash statistics but come to opposite conclusions. Which interpretation of the statistics do you find more persuasive? Citing from the viewpoints, explain your answer.

3. What commonalities can you find in the views expressed by authors that oppose the recommended transportation safety laws in the chapter? Citing from the viewpoints, explain.

Chapter 4

1. Which of the technologies explored in this chapter do you think will have the greatest impact on the future of transportation? Explain your answer, citing from the viewpoints.

2. Eric Russell argues that maglev trains are a desirable alternative to traditional railroads. The *Los Angeles Times* claims that the expense makes maglev trains impractical. Which viewpoint do you find more persuasive? Explain.

3. What are some of the common goals of the future transportation technologies explored by the authors in this chapter?

4. What are some of the common challenges the future transportation technologies explored by the authors in this chapter face? Cite from the viewpoints in your answer.

Organizations to Contact

The editors have compiled the following list of organizations concerned with the issues debated in this book. The descriptions are derived from materials provided by the organizations. All have publications or information available for interested readers. The list was compiled on the date of publication of the present volume; the information provided here may change. Be aware that many organizations take several weeks or longer to respond to inquiries, so allow as much time as possible.

Advocates for Highway and Auto Safety
750 First St. NE, Suite 901, Washington, DC   20002
(202) 408-1711 • fax: (202) 408-1699
e-mail: advocates@saferoads.org
Web site: www.saferoads.org

An alliance of consumer, health, safety groups, and insurance companies, Advocates for Highway and Auto Safety seeks to make America's roads safer. The alliance promotes the adoption of federal and state laws, policies, and programs that save lives and reduce injuries. On its Web site the organization publishes fact sheets, press releases, polls, and reports, including *2007 Roadmap to Highway Safety Laws*. The Web site also includes links to legislative reports and testimony on federal legislation involving traffic safety.

Air Transport Association (ATA)
1301 Pennsylvania Ave. NW, Suite 1100
Washington, DC   20004
(202) 626-4000
e-mail: ata@airlines.org
Web site: www.airlines.org

ATA is a trade organization that represents the major U.S. air carriers, promotes aviation safety, and monitors legislation affecting the industry. On its Web site the association publishes press releases, speeches, issue briefs, and testimony, including "Managing Risk and Increasing Efficiency: An Examination of the Implementation of the Registered Traveler Program."

Alliance of Automobile Manufacturers

1401 Eye St. NW, Suite 900, Washington, DC 20005
(202) 326-5500 • fax: (202) 326-5598
Web site: www.autoalliance.org

A coalition of ten car and light-truck manufacturers, including the Big Three U.S. automakers, the alliance provides a forum to advance policies that promote clean, safe, and affordable personal transportation. On its Web site the alliance publishes fact sheets, articles, and reports, including "Event Data Recorders: The Facts & Benefits" and "Alternate Fuel Autos."

American Association of Port Authorities (AAPA)

1010 Duke St., Alexandria, VA 22314
(703) 684-5700 • fax: (703) 684-6321
e-mail: info@aapa-ports.org
Web site: www.aapa-ports.org

The association represents more than 150 port authorities in the United States, Canada, the Caribbean, and Latin America. AAPA publishes the weekly legislative newsletter *Alert*, the weekly digest *Advisory*, and the quarterly magazine *Seaports*, recent issues of which are available on its Web site. On the Web site's Issues & Advocacy link, AAPA publishes articles and testimony on U.S. port security.

American Driver & Traffic Safety Education Association (ADTSEA)

Highway Safety Center, Indiana University of Pennsylvania
    R&P Bldg., Indiana, PA 15705
(724) 357-3975 • fax: (724) 357-7595
e-mail: support@hsc.iup.edu
Web site: http://adtsea.iup.edu

ADTSEA works with driver education instructors and state authorities to improve driver education standards and practices. It also creates and publishes policies and guidelines for the discipline. In its Web site's Resource Library, ADTSEA publishes white papers, articles, and reports, including "Are Driver Education Courses for Teenagers Effective?—YES!" and "Brain Development and Risk-Taking in Adolescent Drivers."

American Hydrogen Association
2350 W. Shangri La, Phoenix, AZ 85029
(602) 328-4238
Web site: www.clean-air.org

The association's mission is to promote interest in the establishment of a renewable hydrogen energy economy by the year 2010. It works in cooperation with environmental groups, industry, communities, and schools to promote understanding of hydrogen technology and help create a marketplace for hydrogen energy. The association publishes the periodic newsletter, *Hydrogen Today*, recent issues of which are available on its Web site.

Bureau of Transportation Statistics (BTS)
400 Seventh St. SW, Rm. 3103, Washington, DC 20590
(202) 366-1270
e-mail: answers@bts.gov
Web site: www.bts.gov

The bureau is a Department of Transportation agency that compiles statistics on all major modes of transportation in the United States to ensure the most cost-effective use of transportation resources. On its Web site, BTS provides data and statistics organized by transportation mode and subject.

Cato Institute
1000 Massachusetts Ave. NW, Washington, DC 20001-5403
(202) 842-0200 • fax: (202) 842-3490
e-mail: cato@cato.org
Web site: www.cato.org

The Cato Institute is a libertarian public policy research foundation that aims to limit the role of government and protect civil liberties. The institute publishes the quarterlies *CATO Journal* and *Regulation* and the bimonthly *Cato Policy Report*. Its Web site publishes selections from these and other publications and Podcasts on energy and transportation policy, including "Is Ethanol the 'Energy Security' Solution?" and "The Power of Ethanol Is No Panacea."

Flight Safety Foundation (FSF)

601 Madison St., Suite 300, Alexandria, VA   22314
(703) 793-6700 • fax: (703) 739-6708
Web site: www.flightsafety.org

Referred to as the "conscience of the industry," the independent Flight Safety Foundation's mission is to improve global aviation safety through research, education, and advocacy. FSF publishes the monthly *Aero Safety World*, recent issues of which are available on its Web site.

Insurance Institute for Highway Safety (IIHS)

1005 N. Glebe Rd., Suite 800, Arlington, VA   22201
(703) 247-1500 • fax: (703) 247-1588
Web site: www.iihs.org

IIHS is a nonprofit research and public information organization funded by auto insurers. The institute conducts research to find effective measures to prevent motor vehicle crashes. On its Web site IIHS publishes information on the results of its research, including press releases and a bibliography of articles on highway safety topics. The institute publishes a newsletter, *Status Report*, the current issue of which is available on the Web site.

International Association for Hydrogen Energy (IAHE)

5783 SW Fortieth St., Suite 303, Miami, FL   33155
e-mail: info@iahe.org
Web site: www.iahe.org

The IAHE is a group of scientists and engineers professionally involved in the production and use of hydrogen. It sponsors international forums to further its goal of creating an energy system based on hydrogen. The association publishes the monthly *International Journal for Hydrogen Energy.*

National Corn Growers Association (NCGA)
632 Cepi Dr., Chesterfield, MO   63005
(636) 733-9004 • fax: (636) 733-9005
e-mail: corninfo@ncga.com
Web site: www.ncga.com

The NCGA is a federation of state organizations, corn boards, councils, and commissions whose goal is to develop and implement programs and policies to help protect and advance the corn producer's interests. The association lobbies on behalf of corn producers to promote the use of corn-based ethanol. On its Web site, NCGA publishes policy papers, issue briefs, and testimony on the benefits of ethanol, including "The Truth About Ethanol—Addressing the Myths of the Pimentel/Patzek Study" and "Big Oil v. Ethanol: The Consumer Stake in Expanding the Production of Liquid Fuels."

National Highway Traffic Safety Administration (NHTSA)
1200 New Jersey Ave. SE, West Bldg.
Washington, DC   20590
(888) 327-4236
Web site: www.nhtsa.dot.gov

An agency of the U.S. Department of Transportation established by the Highway Safety Act of 1970, the NHTSA's function is to reduce deaths, injuries, and economic losses resulting from motor vehicle crashes. The NHTSA sets and enforces safety performance standards for motor vehicles, and through grants to state and local governments, enables them to conduct local highway safety programs. On its Web site, NHTSA publishes fact sheets, articles, and reports on a variety of traffic safety issues, including "Saving Teenage Lives" and "Motorcycle Helmet Effectiveness Revisited."

Renewable Fuels Association (RFA)
One Massachusetts Ave. NW, Suite 820
Washington, DC   20001
(202) 289-3835
e-mail: info@ethanolrfa.org
Web site: www.ethanolrfa.org

A cross-section of businesses, individuals and organizations, RFA researches, produces, and markets renewable fuels. It represents the renewable fuels industry before the federal government and publishes the monthly newsletter, *Ethanol Report.* RFA publishes fact sheets, position papers, studies, and reports, some of which are available on its Web site, including "Fuel Ethanol: A Technological Evolution" and "Over a Barrel: Why Aren't Oil Companies Using Ethanol to Lower Gasoline Prices?"

Transportation Security Administration (TSA)
601 S. Twelfth St., Arlington, VA   22202
(202) 866-9673
Web site: www.tsa.gov

Created following the terrorist attacks of September 11, 2001, the TSA is a component of the Department of Homeland Security and is responsible for the security of the nation's transportation systems. The TSA oversees security for the highways, railroads, buses, mass transit systems, ports, and the 450 U.S. airports. On its Web site the TSA publishes fact sheets, articles, and testimony on airport and other transportation security issues.

Union of Concerned Scientists (UCS)
2 Brattle Square, Cambridge, MA   02238
(617) 547-5552 • fax: (617) 864-9405
e-mail: ucs@ucsusa.org
Web site: www.ucsusa.org

UCS is a nonprofit alliance of scientists who contend that energy alternatives to oil must be developed to reduce pollution and slow global warming. UCS publishes numerous articles and reports on alternative energy sources and ways to reduce fuel consumption, which are available on its Web site.

World Shipping Council
1156 Fifteenth St. NW, Suite 300, Washington, DC   20005
(202) 589-1230 • fax: (202) 589-1231
e-mail: info@worldshipping.org
Web site: www.worldshipping.org

A trade group representing more than forty shipping companies, including the largest container lines, the council provides a voice for the shipping industry when working with global policy makers. Much of its work is devoted to developing programs that improve maritime security without impeding the free flow of commerce. The council publishes speeches, testimony, and regulatory comments on its Web site.

Bibliography

Curtis D. Anderson and Judy Anderson
Electric and Hybrid Cars: A History. Jefferson, NC: McFarland, 2005.

Ceder Avishai
Public Transit Planning and Operation: Theory, Modelling and Practice. London: Elsevier, 2007.

Paula Berinstein
Making Space Happen: Private Space Efforts and the People Behind Them. Medford, NJ: Medford Press, 2002.

Harvey Blatt
America's Environmental Report Card: Are We Making the Grade? Cambridge, MA: MIT Press, 2005.

Godfrey Boyle
Renewable Energy: Power for a Sustainable Future. New York: Oxford University Press, 2004.

Lester Brown
Rescuing a Planet Under Stress and a Civilization in Trouble. New York: Norton, 2003.

Rebecca L. Busby
Hydrogen and Fuel Cells: A Comprehensive Guide. Tulsa, OK: PennWell, 2005

Committee on Assessment of Security Technologies for Transportation
Defending the U.S. Air Transportation System Against Chemical and Biological Threats. Washington, DC: National Academies Press, 2006.

Kenneth F. Deffeyes
Beyond Oil: The View from Hubbert's Peak. New York: Hill & Wang, 2005.

John M. Deutch   *Making Technology Work: Applications in Energy and the Environment.* New York: Cambridge University Press, 2004.

Clark Kent Ervin   *Open Target: Where America Is Vulnerable to Attack.* New York: Palgrave Macmillan, 2006.

Kaitlen Jay Exum and Lynn M. Messina, eds.   *The Car and Its Future.* New York: H.W. Wilson, 2004.

Richard T.T. Forman   *Road Ecology: Science and Solutions.* Washington, DC: Island, 2003.

Mark S. Foster   *A Nation on Wheels: The Automobile Culture in America Since 1945.* Belmont, CA: Wadsworth, 2003.

Ross Gelbspan   *Boiling Point: How Politicians, Big Oil and Coal, Journalists and Activists Are Fueling the Climate Crisis and What We Can Do to Avert Disaster.* New York: Basic Books, 2005.

Jonathan L. Gifford   *Flexible Urban Transportation.* New York: Pergamon, 2003.

David L. Goodstein   *Out of Gas: The End of the Age of Oil.* New York: Norton, 2004.

Owen D. Gutfreund   *Twentieth-Century Sprawl: Highways and the Reshaping of the American Landscape.* New York: Oxford University Press, 2004.

Susan Hanson and Genevieve Giuliano — *The Geography of Urban Transportation.* New York: Guilford, 2004.

Jon D. Haveman and Howard J. Shatz, eds. — *Protecting the Nation's Seaports: Balancing Security and Cost.* San Francisco: Public Policy Institute of California, 2006.

David F. Hennessy — *Clearing a Road to Driving Fitness by Better Assessing Driving Wellness.* Sacramento: California Dept. of Motor Vehicles, Research and Development Section, 2005.

Michael Frank Hordeski — *Alternative Fuels: The Future of Hydrogen.* Lilburn, GA: Fairmont, 2007.

Peter W. Huber and Mark P. Mills — *The Bottomless Well: The Twilight of Fuel, the Virtue of Waste, and Why We Will Never Run Out of Energy.* New York: Basic Books, 2005.

Edward L. Hudgins — *Space: The Free-Market Frontier.* Washington, DC: Cato Institute, 2003.

Mark Jaccard — *Sustainable Fossil Fuels: The Unusual Suspect in the Quest for Clean and Enduring Energy.* Cambridge: Cambridge University Press, 2005.

Michael T. Klare — *Blood and Oil: The Dangers and Consequences of America's Growing Dependency on Imported Petroleum.* New York: Metropolitan, 2004.

Paul Komor — *Renewable Energy Policy.* Lincoln, NE: iUniverse, 2004.

Elizabeth Kopits   *Why Have Traffic Fatalities Declined in Industrialized Countries? Implications for Pedestrians and Vehicle Occupants.* Washington, DC: World Bank, Development Research Group, Infrastructure and Environment Team, 2005.

Michelle Kubik   *Consumer Views on Transportation and Energy.* Golden, CO: National Renewable Energy Laboratory, 2005.

National Highway Traffic Safety Administration   *Cruisin' Without Bruisin'.* Washington, DC: U.S. Dept. of Transportation, 2004.

Dom Nozzi   *Road to Ruin: An Introduction to Sprawl and How to Cure It.* Westport, CT: Praeger, 2003.

Benjamin Ofori-Amoah   *Beyond the Metropolis: Urban Geography as If Small Cities Mattered.* Lanham, MD: University Press of America, 2007.

Greg Pahl   *Biodiesel: Growing a New Energy Economy.* White River Junction, VT: Chelsea Green, 2005.

Joseph M. Pellerito et al.   *Driver Rehabilitation and Community Mobility: Principles and Practice.* St. Louis, MO: Elsevier Mosby, 2006.

Paul Roberts   *The End of Oil: On the Edge of a Perilous New World.* New York: Houghton Mifflin, 2004.

Mark H. Rose, Bruce E. Seely, and Paul F. Barrett	*The Best Transportation System in the World: Railroads, Trucks, Airlines, and American Public Policy in the Twentieth Century.* Columbus: Ohio State University Press, 2006.
Paul Schilperoord	*Future Tech: Innovations in Transportation.* London: Black Dog, 2006.
Joseph M. Sussman	*Perspectives on Intelligent Transportation Systems (ITS).* New York: Springer Science+Business Media, 2005.
James A. Vedda	*Study of the Liability Risk-Sharing Regime in the United States for Commercial Space Transportation.* El Segundo, CA: Aerospace Corp., 2006.

Index